Guy Debord

Titles in the series Critical Lives present the work of leading cultural figures of the modern period. Each book explores the life of the artist, writer, philosopher or architect in question and relates it to their major works.

In the same series

Michel Foucault
David Macey

Jean Genet
Stephen Barber

Pablo Picasso
Mary Ann Caws

Franz Kafka
Sander L. Gilman

Guy Debord

Andy Merrifield

REAKTION BOOKS

Pour Corinna, comme d'hab'

Published by Reaktion Books Ltd
33 Great Sutton Street
London EC1V 0DX, UK

www.reaktionbooks.co.uk

First published 2005

Printed and bound in Great Britain
by CPI/Bath Press, Bath

British Library Cataloguing in Publication Data
Merrifield, Andy
    Guy Debord. – (Critical lives)
    1. Debord, Guy, 1931– 2. Internationale situationniste
    3. Radicals – France – Biography
    I. Title
    303.4'84'092

ISBN: 1 86189 261 6

Contents

La nuit, lorsque l'aquilon ébranlait ma chaumière . . . il me semblait que la vie redoublait au fond de mon cœur, que j'aurais la puissance de créer des mondes.

Chateaubriand, *René*

1

Eyes for Blowing Up Bridges

What acceptable paradise can we extract from so many ruins,
Hervé, without falling into them?
Guy Debord, *Le Marquis de Sade a des yeux de fille*

Bellevue-la-Montagne is a sleepy, almost-deserted village perched
on a 1,000-metre hillock in the northern reaches of France's Haute-
Loire. Up here, looking south-east, there is a fine view of mountains, of the Massif Central, whose flat-topped volcanoes dominate
this part of the rugged Auvergne. Volcanoes are everywhere and
stretch as far as the eye can see. Scattered amid them, around
every side of Bellevue, are numerous tiny hamlets, many made
up of just two or three houses, replete with a few clucking hens
and barking dogs. About a kilometre further north along the
D906, motorists reach a sign indicating one of them: CHAMPOT.

After a sharp right turn, a narrow lane leads you to another
signpost, and to another sharp right turn down an even narrower
lane. After a minute the track suddenly dips and the vista ahead
allows you to glimpse an earlier age, a pre-modern France, more
Villon than Flaubert, with battalions of trees and seemingly endless meadows, a patchwork quilt of every shade of green under
the sun. In the immediate foreground are a cluster of five modest
cottages, Champot Haut; one property, to the far left, is surrounded by a high wall made up of light-tanned boulders, which
renders the house within only partly visible, giving it an air of

On the road to Champot.

mystery. Only the outside mailbox, still adorned with the name of
its late resident and his widow, offers clues to this mystery:
'DEBORD • BECKER-HO'.

The former occupant of the house was himself somewhat mysterious. He'd lived inside these walls with his wife Alice Becker-Ho
on and off for almost twenty years. He'd spent most of his summers and occasional winters here. But on 30 November 1994, late
on a drizzly afternoon, he'd ended it all. The rumour then, since
substantiated, was that he'd meticulously used a single bullet to
shoot himself through the heart. He was dying anyway, of an
alcohol-related illness, peripheral neuritis, which gradually burned
away the body's nerve endings and brought on excruciating pain,
apparently too much pain to endure.

The regional newspaper, *La Tribune – Le Progrès*, devoted a brief
column to the incident on 2 December: 'Writer and filmmaker
Guy Debord, father of Situationism and master of subversion,
killed himself on Wednesday evening, at the age of 62, in his
domicile of Champot, in the Bellevue-la-Montagne commune.'
In Parisian intellectual circles, however, it was front-page news,
the headline of the next day's *Le Monde*: Guy Debord, 'aesthete

The Debord/ Becker-Ho postbox.

of subversion' and 'theoretician of "the society of the spectacle"', was dead. Inside, there was an entire page spread, a tribute-cum-critique of the man who'd fled Paris in 1970 to become ever more reclusive and elusive.

Guy Debord's house at Champot.

Who was this man I'd wandered through a time-warp searching for? Who was this man journalists and critics variously labelled 'mastermind, nihilist, pseudo-philosopher, pope, loner, mentor, hypnotist, self-obsessed fanatic, devil, *éminence grise*, damned soul, professor of radicalism, guru, mad sadist, cynic, cheap Mephisto, bewitcher, fearsome destabilizer'?[1] Moreover, how could somebody who had become infamous in 1967 for a cult book, *The Society of the Spectacle*, for his part in the May 1968 insurrections, for drunken binges and late-night wanderings in Paris during the 1950s and '60s, for city street-smarts and Marxist pretensions – how could he somehow flee the city, flee modern life itself, and live in isolation in this rural fortress? It had been a strange, Rimbaudesque voyage for Debord; only instead of eloping to Africa never to write again, Debord escaped to an unlikely Haute-Loire, and wrote infrequently. In the Haute-Loire, he said, he'd savoured 'the pleasures of exile as others suffered the pains of submission'.[2] The key to understanding Guy Debord lay not in the grubby backstreets of Paris, nor in the smoky bars where the Situationists' raw, unfettered radicalism was hatched. The real Debord resides on the other side of that wall, at Champot, where a solitary, aging recluse plotted to overthrow the world in his head.

The high wall around Debord's house in Champot was chosen intentionally. It emphasized a kind of fortress, a refuge inside ramparts, a utility brilliantly delineated by the master philosopher and tactician of war, Karl von Clausewitz, whose *On War* (1832–7) was much scrutinized by the aging revolutionary. (It was a text that equally impressed Marx and Engels, as well as Lenin, Trotsky and Mao.) 'A noble who was hard pressed on all sides', Clausewitz wrote, 'fled to his castle in order to gain time and wait for a better turn of events. By their fortifications . . . [they] sought to ward off the storm clouds of war.'[3] Debord saw himself as such a noble and considered Champot his defence against assault.

Debord's board-game Kriegspiel (from Debord's film *In Girum Imus Nocte Et Consumimur Igni*).

For a lifetime, Guy Debord kept his enemy under observation. For a lifetime, revolutionary practice had been akin to warlike strategizing, each the domain of danger and disappointment. In Champot, Debord ruminated on war, on its theory and actual history, spending quiet, lonely summer days studying real battles, reading up on the logic of war, not only by Clausewitz, but also Machiavelli, Sun Tzu and Thucydides. There are books one loves to meditate on in voluntary exile, in the course of a life of intrigue and obscurity. In voluntary exile, Debord even invented his own war board game, *Kriegspiel*. 'I succeeded, a long time ago,' he said,

> in presenting the basics of [war's] movements on a rather simple board game: the forces in contention and the contradictory necessities imposed on the operations of each of the two parties. I have played this game and in the often difficult conduct of my life, I have utilized information from it – I have also set myself rules of the game for this life, and I have followed them . . . On the question of whether I have made good use of such lessons, I will leave it to others to decide.[4]

This present book will attempt to get over that high Champot wall, peer inside Debord's house, push back its shutters, drink his wine and listen to him talk. What follows is a tale of a free spirit who was radically at odds with life but who loved a lot of things in life and thought them worth fighting for. It is a story, in Homer's words, 'singing of a man and Muse, a man of twists and turns driven time and again off course', about a man who had lived life to the full, who had loved fine wine, intelligent conversation, attractive company and a few stimulating books, things that seemed so obvious and simple yet are difficult to find. In fact, today, said Debord, 'the more simple things always seem closer to the critique of society'.[5]

In *Panégyrique*, his slim autobiography of 1989, a masterpiece of sangfroid *belles-lettres*, Guy Debord is measured, elegant and often self-deprecating. There, he reveals 'what I had loved'.[6] It's clear he had loved many books, many writers, and had read a lot: Sterne, Clausewitz, Li Po, Dante, Cardinal de Retz, Omar Khayyám, Machiavelli, Cravan, Lautréamont, Thucydides, Sun Tzu, Marx, Castiglione, Villon, Tocqueville, Gracián, Orwell, De Quincey, Brenan, Mac Orlan, Saint-Simon, Swift, Borrow, Manrique, Hegel, Feuerbach, Lukacs, etc., etc. He'd also told us of his love for 'the real Spain', for Italy, and for a Paris that was no more; he had loved not a few women, too, especially Alice; he had loved his murdered friend Gérard Lebovici; and, perhaps above all, he had loved to drink. 'Even though I have read a lot, I have drunk even more. I have written much less than most people who write; but I have drunk much more than most people who drink.'[7]

The mature Debord increasingly came to resemble Geoffrey Fermin, the doomed Consul, the anti-hero of Malcolm Lowry's *Under the Volcano* (1947), a novel the youthful Debord had greatly admired.[8] With a tragic cast, Debord would similarly brood, under Auvergne's volcanoes. And, like the Consul, he loved the magnificent and terrible peace that alcohol induced. 'Nothing in the world was more terrible than an empty bottle!' the Consul said. 'Unless it was an empty glass.'[9] 'How, unless you drink as I do', he says elsewhere, 'can you hope to understand the beauty of an old woman from

Tarasco who plays dominoes at seven o'clock in the morning?'[10] 'I would have had very few illnesses', Debord wrote, 'if alcohol had not in the end brought me some: from insomnia to vertigo, by way of gout . . . There are mornings that are stirring but difficult.'[11] Life itself, Debord always insisted, should be a kind of intoxication, a majestic and fertile river that he wanted passionately to consume.

In *Panégyrique*, Debord also wrote lovingly about his sojourns in Champot. The 'charm and harmony' of his seasons there hadn't escaped him. It was a 'grandiose isolation', a 'pleasing and impressive solitude'.

> I spent several winters there. Snow fell for days on end. The wind piled it up in drifts . . . Despite the exterior walls, snow accumulated in the courtyard. Logs burned in the fireplace. The house seemed to open directly onto the Milky Way. At night, the nearby stars would shine brilliantly one moment, and the next be extinguished by the passing mist. And so too our conversations and our celebrations, our meetings and our tenacious passions. It was a land of storms. They approached noiselessly at first, announced by a brief passage of a wind that slithered through the grass or by a series of sudden flashes on the horizon; then thunder and lightening unleashed, and we were bombarded for a long time, and from every direction, as if in a fortress under siege. One time, at night, I saw lightning strike near me, outside: you could not even see where it had struck; the whole landscape was equally illuminated for a startling instant. Nothing in art seemed to give me this impression of an irrevocable brilliance, except for the prose that Lautréamont employed in the programmatic exposition that he called *Poésies*.[12]

Debord himself was something of a prophet of storms and violent winds: he'd lived through a lot of them, and conjured up a few more in his own imagination. 'All my life', he began *Panégyrique*,

'I have seen only troubled times, extreme divisions in society, and immense destruction; I have taken part in these troubles.' He had lived through 'an era when so many things have changed at the astounding speed of catastrophes, in which almost every point of reference and measure suddenly got swept away, along with the ground on which it was built.' Little wonder

> I saw around me a great number of individuals who died young, and not always by suicide, frequent as that was. On the matter of violent death, I remark, without being able to advance a fully rational explanation of the phenomenon, that the number of my friends who have been killed by bullets constitutes an unusually high percentage.[13]

Yet for locals of Champot and Bellevue, Monsieur Debord was a rather reserved, distant character, seldom going out, and taciturn when he did. On odd occasions, dressed in black, donned in his seaman's cap – his *casquette de marine* – arm-in-arm with Alice, he walked with his cane into Bellevue. Madame Soulier, in Bellevue's *boucherie*, recalls Debord in the 1980s lunching at the now-extinct restaurant, Le Midi, next door to her store. He was fairly short and fat, she said, with a big stomach and glasses. He'd often buy meat from her for their evening meal. He'd come in with his wife, 'Madame Becker', 'a Eurasian', who was always polite and still returns to Champot every summer, in July and August.

Alice Becker-Ho was Debord's second wife, whom he married in 1972 after divorcing Michèle Bernstein, an earlier flame and a fellow founder of the Situationist International. Alice's mother, a Shanghai native, had married a German, Wolf Becker, who'd been a deserter from the Reich army. The Becker-Ho family settled in Paris, in rue de la Montagne-Sainte-Geneviève, close to the Cluny Museum, where mother Becker-Ho ran a Chinese restaurant.

Alice's brother, Eugene Becker-Ho, a Paris antiques dealer, who also has a big country manor in Saint-Pierre-du-Mont, Normandy, and a stable of horses, owns Debord's Champot Haut house.

Sometimes Guy and Alice had guests down from Paris. Sports cars would park in front of the wall, and action inside the house heated up at night when the Debords entertained, cooking sumptuous meals and drinking fine wine. In those days, there were other, less-welcome visitors to Champot: journalists and paparazzi – eager for an off-guard shot of Debord, something they could sell to a glossy *hebdomadaire* – and La Direction de la Surveillance du Territoire (DST), the French secret police, who had kept tabs on the legendary subversive since 1968, believing him connected to the Italian militant Red Brigade and the German Baader-Meinhof Gang.[14] Champot was his base, his stronghold, from where he'd plot to overthrow European governments, plant bombs and kidnap prominent politicians – or so it was thought. Debord scoffed at their bungling incompetence. He viewed journalists and police as he viewed bothersome flies in summer.[15] He'd close the property's shutters to ward both off.

The DST also kept close watch on the Chinese restaurant of Alice's mother, suspecting that Chinese Communist Party agents ate there, and that it was the hatching-place of all sorts of Fu Manchu plots. Debord put the record straight: he was, he said, never involved with any Communist organizations, nor with Left political figures or even the intellectuals of his day. In fact, he said, 'I have firmly kept myself apart from all semblance of participation in the circles that then passed for intellectual or artistic.'[16]

I have lived comfortably among the lowest levels of society, among the Kabyles in Paris, surrounded by Gypsies, always in good company. In brief, I have lived everywhere except amongst the intellectuals of this era. This is naturally because I despise them; and who, knowing their complete works, will be surprised?[17]

Debord's defiance was like that of Dostoevsky's underground man: he carried to an extreme what others did not dare to carry halfway. 'I have tasted pleasures', he said, 'little known to people who have obeyed the unfortunate laws of this era.'[18]

A self-proclaimed 'doctor of nothing', Guy Louis Marie Vincent Ernest Debord was born in 1931 in a peripheral quarter of Paris, the rundown La Mouzaïa in the 20th *arrondissement*. His bourgeois family's fortune, he claimed, was wiped out in the 1930s as economic crisis swept eastwards from America. Thereafter, in the course of adolescence, 'I had simply not attached any sort of importance to those rather abstract questions about the future.' 'I went slowly but inevitably', he said, 'toward a life of adventure, with my eyes open. I could not even think of studying for one of the learned professions that lead to holding down a job, for all of them seemed completely alien to my tastes or contrary to my opinions.'[19]

Debord seldom disclosed much about his past. His family, on his mother's side, may have been wealthier than he claimed. But we can assume that his childhood was not entirely happy; his past may have been a bit like young Stephen Dedalus's, entering the world to seek misfortune. His father died of tuberculosis when he was four. Guy, who'd been diagnosed asthmatic, his mother Paulette and grandmother Lydie 'Manou' moved south just before war broke out, to Nice, outside the Occupied Zone. There, Paulette tried her best to keep the family together. The two women adored Guy, and he was no doubt spoilt and doted upon. Soon, though, Paulette had a fling with an Italian driving instructor, and gave birth to Guy's half-sister, Michèle Dominique, in 1942. That same year, the extended family moved west to Pau, an elegant resort in the foothills of the Pyrenees, and settled in the centre of town. Guy enrolled at Pau's *lycée* (now the Lycée Louis-Barthou), where he became a rather solitary, precocious child, insecure and arrogant, reading a lot of adventure stories and poetry.

By a quirky coincidence, one of his poet idols, Isidore Ducasse, aka the Comte de Lautréamont, had attended the very same school back in 1863. Several years later, Lautréamont had published *Les Chants de Maldoror* (1869) and *Poésies* (1870), two mad hallucinatory visions, proto-Surrealist classics, at once beautiful and grotesque. Less than a year after *Poésies*, Lautréamont was dead, at the age of 24. Debord loved Lautréamont's in-your-face subversion; one dissatisfied youth recognized another. 'The poetic whimperings of this century', *Poésies* begin, 'are nothing but sophistry.' Debord never stopped loving Lautréamont and always paid homage to the true inventor of *détournement*, a favoured pastime the Situationists would later utilize.[20] Part II of *Poésies* had 'inverted' a host of famous verses and maxims by Pascal, Hugo, Kant *et al.* The more rational the reversals, said Debord in an essay of 1959, 'Methods of *Détournement*', the less effective the *détournement*. Lautréamont wrote only at night, seated at a piano, drinking absinthe. The taciturn poet hammered out words at the same time as he hammered out notes, much to his neighbour's chagrin. His meagre oeuvre defied any classification.

Maldoror was neither novel nor prose-poem: it followed no linear path, often switched tenses, went from singular to plural, and wilfully ignored punctuation. It was a flight of fancy, a dream, a hallucination, a mental derangement, an epic odyssey of Maldoror, the 'prince of darkness', who cursed God and hailed the 'old ocean'. Maldoror, Lautréamont said, is a bandit who 'is, perhaps, seven leagues from this land' or 'perhaps he is some steps from you'.[21] *Maldoror* was seen as blasphemous; prospective publishers feared litigation. For a while it was banned. Now, it has been accepted into the French canon, infamous for lines that became touchstones of the Surrealist movement: 'the fortuitous meeting on a dissection table of a sewing machine and an umbrella'.[22] Elsewhere came scattered, deliberately opaque similes: 'beautiful like the law of arrested development in the chest of adults whose propensity for growth

Debord aged 19, from his film *In Girum Imus Nocte Et Consumimur Igni.*

isn't in rapport with the quantity of molecules that their organism assimilates'; 'beautiful like the congenital malformation of a man's sexual organs'. And one that Debord loved to recite, 'beautiful like the trembling of the hands in alcoholism'.[23]

Poésies was the sober counterpart to the ravings of *Maldoror*, its moral antidote, its negation and subversion – its *détournement*. Lautréamont himself may have been a schizophrenic, and side-by-side the works evoke a Jekyll and Hyde persona. *Poésies* is famed for the maxim that became sacred to Debord and the Situationists, who'd soon enough rip off and lampoon many 'great' works and ideas: 'Plagiarism is necessary', Lautréamont insisted, 'progress implies it. It tightly squeezes an author's phrase, serves his expression, erases a false idea, replaces it with a just notion.'[24]

Debord's initiation to the writings of another enduring influence, Arthur Cravan, came a little before his encounter with an almost real-life Isidore Ducasse; an eccentric Romanian bohemian, Isidore Isou, poet and guru of the Lettrist movement, whom Debord met at the Cannes Film Festival of 1951. After the Liberation of France, the Debord family left Pau for the chic Côte d'Azur town of Cannes where Guy attended the Lycée Carnot. He showed little interest in anything there. Though he once won a prize in a radio general knowledge quiz, Guy didn't excel. He read things that didn't appear on the curriculum and instead of his homework wrote long, meticulously crafted letters, full of effusive poetry and revolutionary idealism, to a school pal Hervé Falcou, two years his junior: 'We have been *enfants terribles*', said one outpouring, a chip off Rimbaud's block. 'If we become adults we will be dangerous men.' 'An individual ought to be passionate or he is nothing', affirmed another. 'The Marquis de Sade has young girl's eyes. Beautiful eyes for blowing up bridges . . . '.[25]

Young Guy yearned for something else, for another world, and caught a glimpse of it at the town's fourth film festival soon after he'd finished his *baccalauréat*. It was Isou and the crazy rebellious world he created that really lit Debord's fire. The Lettrists, who'd journeyed down from Paris, sported turtleneck sweaters and jeans and dug jazz. They were hip and Debord hadn't seen their like before. Isou himself usually donned a silk cravat and was a curious mix of bourgeois elegance and rumpled decadence. He was a sleazy reincarnation of Lautréamont and Rimbaud. He and his disciples were at Cannes to promote an offbeat film, *Treatise on Slime and Eternity*, and to stir up trouble. They intended to upstage the conventional film world; Debord towed along, engaging in rowdy alcoholic binges. Isou's film caused an uproar: nothing happened; a blank screen often prevailed, interspersed with bizarre, guttural noises masquerading as poetry; and it lasted for more than four hours . . .

After Cannes, Isou helped Debord find a small furnished room in Paris at the Hôtel de la Faculté on the rue Racine. Debord told his mother he planned to enroll at the Sorbonne to pursue a law degree, for which she'd send him a modest monthly sum. He enrolled yet did little conventional studying. With his membership of the university, he could borrow books from the Sorbonne library and get a discount on meals at nearby restaurants and canteens. So he read a lot, smoked, drank, flirted with women, and posed as a struggling Left Bank student. Dada and Surrealist texts became his staple, and Debord's appetite for adventure and carousing got whetted by a certain poet, boxer and wild man deserter of seventeen nations, Arthur Cravan.

If Lautréamont's output was slim, Arthur Cravan's was even slimmer. Born Fabian Avenarius Lloyd in 1887 in the genteel Swiss town of Lausanne, Cravan carried a British passport yet preferred to speak French. A human chameleon, he never identified with any place in particular, and often masqueraded behind forged papers, claiming all the while to be Oscar Wilde's nephew. (As the son of the notorious scribe's brother-in-law, this was one piece of bombast that was actually true.) At a height of 6 ft 7 in (2 m) and weighing 265 lb (120 kg), Cravan was built like the Eiffel Tower and held the European heavyweight title for a brief period.

In 1916, he fought the ex-world champion, Jack Johnson, in Barcelona, in a rigged fight, a spectacular ploy to earn the penniless Cravan sufficient for steerage to New York, where the boxer-poet-cum-conscientious objector could avoid military service. Cravan tumbled in the sixth round, amid a delirious and suspecting crowd, who simultaneously chanted and booed when he didn't get up. A riot ensued; Cravan slipped out of a side exit and soon set sail on the *Montserrat* across a storm-tossed ocean, alongside a motley crew of deserters, adventurers and dissidents, as well as a certain Leon Trotsky.

Cravan was happiest wandering: 'I have twenty countries in my memory and trail in my soul the colours of one hundred cities.'[26] He could only feel himself, he said, 'in voyage; when I stay a long time in the same place, stupidity overwhelms me.' Cravan was a shameless exhibitionist and self-promoter, and had a habit of dancing on tables and pulling down his trousers. He managed to start up a pesky little journal, *Maintenant*, which advertised soirées of poetry readings and boxing instruction. Only six issues appeared; Cravan was editor-in-chief and sole contributor, often penning diatribes under pseudonyms such as W. Cooper and Robert Miradique. 'Every great artist', Cravan proclaimed – and Debord concurred –

'has the sense of provocation'. 'The letter of insult is a sort of literary genre that held a grand place in our century,' Debord wrote in *Considérations sur l'assassinat de Gérard Lebovici*, 'and not without good reason . . . On this point, I have learnt a lot from the Surrealists and, above all, from Arthur Cravan.'[27] 'Cravan's actions during those few years', the Surrealist king-pin André Breton claimed, 'developed in an atmosphere of absolute irreverence, of provocation and scandal that herald "Dada".' Breton knew that Cravan had 'accomplished, without compromise, Rimbaud's desire: "Il faut être absolument moderne".'[28]

New York dazzled Cravan: 'New York! New York! I should like to inhabit you!' There, he scribbled a few stanzas in a minor literary review called *The Soil*; but in a land where 'science married itself to industry' in 'an audacious modernity', poetry was hardly an earner. Broke, he drank in dive bars in the Bronx and slept rough in Central Park, until he met and later married the English poet and artist Mina Loy. (She wrote a touching memoir about him called *Colossus*.) In 1918 they moved to Mexico City, where Cravan became a professor of boxing at the School of Physical Culture. He and Loy planned to go to Buenos Aires, but only had enough money for her passage. Cravan decided to navigate himself with a friend in a small fishing boat; he and Loy would rendezvous later in Valparaíso. She waved her 31-year-old husband off one morning late in 1918, from a small pier, and watched the craft breeze out into the open sea. It dipped on the horizon and nobody ever saw Cravan again. Loy bore his daughter, Fabienne, in April 1919.

Debord, unlike Cravan, never visited New York. He was invited there once, in 1959, by his friend Alex Trocchi, who lived for a while on a barge moored on the Hudson at 33rd Street. (Trocchi, a Scot and a junkie, who would have loose affiliations with the Situationists in Paris during the 1950s, had just completed *Cain's Book*, his furtive portrayal of heroin addiction and existential angst, destined to become a bestseller.) Yet Debord turned the invitation down; an American voyage wasn't possible, he said, pointing out the steady work he had to do in Europe.[29] In fact, Debord never ventured beyond Europe and never flew in a plane. His adventures always seemed closer to home and were less exotic: imaginative leaps of the mind and spirit, intellectual and political as much as geographical, taking to the pen and bottle as much as to the high seas.

In *Panégyrique*, he admitted: 'I haven't had the need to travel very far.' 'Most of the time I lived in Paris, exactly in the triangle defined by the intersections of the rue Saint-Jacques and the rue Royer-Colland, rue Saint Martin and rue Greneta, and the rue du Bac and rue de Commailles.'[30] It was a smallish area, accessible on foot, spanning both sides of the Seine, between Les Halles and the Pantheon, in the 3rd and 5th *arrondissements*. He had, he said, spent his days and nights in this zone, and never would have left if the life he'd led there hadn't been completely destroyed. 'Soon', Debord lamented years later, citing Arthur Cravan as testimony, 'we will only see artists in the street, and it will take no end of effort to find a single man.'[31]

Throughout the 1950s, this patch became Debord's 'zone of perdition', 'where his youth went as if to achieve its education'.[32] There, without conventional education or grooming, he became an autodidact in every sense, whose life in books was equally books in life. 'I too grew up in the streets', Debord said, citing Aristophanes' *Knights* approvingly. In the streets, bars and libraries, he taught himself what to read and how to act, and how to combine each. His formative milieu, he said, was the 'milieu of demolition experts'[33] and 'dangerous classes', of malcontents and the poor. They engaged in perilous pursuits; devotees had to know how to live off the land – the urban land. They were lost prophets of an age of innocence and *naïveté* and mad, raving ideals. It was an epoch dramatized by what Debord had daubed in chalk in 1953 on a wall along the rue de Seine: *Ne travaillez jamais* ('never work').

It was also an epoch that came to the page in the wonderfully zany text *Mémoires*. 'The rare works of my youth', Debord wrote in a retrospective preface, 'had been special. It is necessary to admit that a taste for generalized negation united them. It was in great harmony with real life that we led then.'[34] Consisting of *structures portantes* ('supporting structures') – contorted cartoons and captions that Debord and the Danish artist Asger Jorn purloined in 1958 – *Mémoires* is a classic piece of *détournement*, 'composed of elements entirely prefabricated', a garish collage of photographs, drawings, sketches and citations sacred and profane, original and ripped off. Some images are straight out of Jackson Pollock, spontaneous outpourings of red, blue and black ink seeping over the page, overlaid with assorted snippets: 'It is the act of a subject profoundly inebriated by alcohol'; 'all the world's twenty-year-olds had genius'; 'we ate well there and met lots of people: writers, artists, more or less poor, and all full of illusions.'

This motley coterie was the most marginal of marginal dissidents; little of their political activity extended beyond a Paris, Amsterdam and Brussels triangle. Their programme was epigrammatic not systematic, bequeathing only scraps and preliminary ideas, vague hypotheses and blurry vignettes. No completed or coherent body of work endures. And yet somehow, after the Situationists, Marxism, urban politics, radical art and design, the status quo, nothing would ever be quite the same again. The saga of the Situationists is full of acronyms and bad faith, whirlwind romances and intense camaraderie, back-stabbing and ideological expulsions. As is so often the case in Left history, everyone seems harder on themselves and their fellow travellers than they do on their ruling-class antagonists. Debord was culpable here, more than most. He was brilliant yet ruthless, seductive yet manipulative, both theoretical mastermind and chief executioner.

Debord, Michèle Bernstein and Asger Jorn.

Situationist prehistory involved several small, subversive avant-garde movements. First came the Lettrist International, Isou's underground minimalist set-up, founded in 1946; but as the 1950s unfolded, it crystallized around Debord, Michèle Bernstein (his first wife) and Gil Wolman. Next was COBRA, the Copenhagen, Brussels and Amsterdam Surrealist and experimental design conglomerate, dominated by the Dutch utopian architect, ex-Provo and anarchist Constant Nieuwenhuys – later abbreviated to the snappier Constant. Soon the Imaginist Bauhaus entered the fray, Asger Jorn's brainchild, with its Abstract Expressionist bent, and London's Psychogeographical Association, with the painter Ralph Rumney, the sole Brit on the scene.

All these groups were highly politicized and revolutionary in their intent to renew art – or, better, to 'abolish' art, much as Karl Marx sought to abolish philosophy – and to renew the action of art on life (and life on art), transforming both in the process. They were bored with art as they knew it, bored with politicians, bored with the city, and bored in the city. The city had become banal, as had art and politics. Banalization was a mental and material disease afflicting life in general. Everything needed changing: life, time and space, cities. Everyone was hypnotized by production and conveniences, by sewage systems, lifts, bathrooms and washing machines. Presented with the choice between love and a garbage disposal unit, Debord quipped, young people opted for garbage disposal units. Baron Haussmann's Paris, the Paris of *grands boulevards* and speedy traffic arteries, 'is a city built by an idiot, full of sound and fury, signifying nothing. Today's urbanism's main problem is ensuring the smooth circulation of a rapidly increasing quantity of motor vehicles.'[35]

The Lettrist International (LI) pushed for new forms of collective expression, including self-expression, and especially irreverent expression; the group embodied the spirit and gusto that would animate and dramatize the Situationists. To begin with, LI members found sustenance from Surrealism and Breton; by the 1950s they thought Surrealism washed up, effete, and lurched instead towards the earlier, more iconoclastic Dada. (Dada's lampooning, its technique of turning images, art and life around, of formulating new meanings from old worn-out meanings and transforming them into shocking, original collages, would become a cherished Situationist practice.)

The LI, meanwhile, pioneered their own shoestring journal, *Potlatch*, named after the great feasts of northwestern Native American tribes. In them, chiefs actually gave food, drink and wealth away; all surpluses were wilfully destroyed. Potlatches forbade bargaining, affirmed gifts, defied 'exchange' and were absolute negations of private property and capitalist values. Debord loved the idea, developing it from the sociologist Marcel Mauss's text of 1925, *The Gift*. Debord drafted numerous polemical pieces for *Potlatch* in the already icy-cool clinical speak he'd make legendary in the decades to follow. 'Our ambitions are clearly megalomaniacal', he wrote in issue 29, 'but perhaps not measurable by the dominant criteria of success. I believe that my friends would satisfy themselves working anonymously in the capacity of a paid worker in the Ministry of Leisure of a government who in the end will be preoccupied by changing life.'[36]

It was as a Lettrist that Debord also launched his first experimental film, *Howlings in Favour of Sade* (*Hurlements en faveur de Sade*, 1952). It set a Debordian movie precedent, after Isou: there would be hardly anything going on, with intermittent periods of silence and darkened frames. Images would suddenly intersperse with monotonous voice-overs, frequently Debord's own. 'There's no film. Cinema is dead', said one in *Howlings*. 'There can't be any more film. If you want, let's have a debate.'[37] Cinema – or anti-cinema – was Debord's first love; he often identified himself as a particular kind of filmmaker. His denunciations of bourgeois cinema also extended to rants against the avant-garde, especially the 'respected' avant-garde like Jean-Luc Godard. In Godard, Debord said, 'the repetition of the same clumsy stupidities is confounded by postulate'. Godard's critique, he added, 'never surpasses the basic humour of a cabaret'.[38]

Howlings entered the limelight as cinematic anti-cinema. 'An important squad of Lettrists', one voice utters, 'constituting thirty members, all donned in a dirty uniform which is their only truly original trademark, will unload at the Croisette with the firmly decreed desire of indulging in some scandal capable of drawing attention to themselves.'[39] 'Happiness is a new idea in Europe', says another. Then, towards the film's end:

'I have nothing more to say to you./ After all the responses at inopportune moments, and youth getting older, night falls again from on high./ SILENCE FOR THREE MINUTES, DURING WHICH THE SCREEN STAYS DARK./ We live as lost children, our adventures incomplete./ SILENCE FOR TWENTY-FOUR MINUTES,

One of the most enduring ideas from *Howlings* was a throw-away refrain: 'The art of the future will be the shattering of situations or nothing.' Indeed, it was around this notion of 'situations' that in July 1957, in a bar in a remote Italian village called Cosio d'Arroscia, Debord and delegates from assorted fringe organizations met 'in a state of semi-drunkenness'. Present at the proceedings, representing the International Lettrists, were Debord and Bernstein, Asger Jorn, Guiseppe Pinot-Gallizio, Walter Olmo; Elena Verrone and Piero Simondo propped up the Imaginist Bauhaus's flank; Ralph Rumney, with his girlfriend Pegeen Guggenheim in tow, did their bit for London's Psychogeographical Association. There and then, by five votes to one, with two abstentions, the Situationist International (SI) became a historical fact; a 25-year-old Debord assumed the mantle of power, demolishing all opposition, friend and foe alike, who would almost immediately feel the wrath of his penchant for expulsion. 'To the door' went 'the old guard' like Isou, whose 'ambitions are too limited' and whose 'individual morality retrograde'.[41] So, too, would go Rumney later for failing to deliver a report on Venice's psychogeography. (It would eventually surface half a century later as a photographic novel called *The Leaning Tower of Venice*.)

The SI reacted against bourgeois culture and politics on the one hand and the sterile, austere functionalism of high modernism on the other. Henceforth they engineered a concerted attack on two fronts. Bourgeois and modernist high culture eviscerated the city; each left its debilitating imprint on the built environment and on social space; each was pathological to the human spirit and to genuine freedom. In the modern city, Logos had triumphed over Eros, order over disorder, organization over rebels. And the old Communist Eastern bloc cities were reviled as much as their capitalist counterparts.

Debord and fellow Situationists in Munich, 1959 (from left to right: Har Oudejans, Constant, Guy Debord and Armando).

Le Corbusier's machine aesthetic and 'Radiant' utopia likewise received the thumbs down, as did the rigid brutalism of the Congress of Modern Architects (CIAM). Ditto the notorious *grands ensembles* barrack blocks; ditto Oscar Niemeyer's Brasilia, touted as one of the pinnacles of the Modern Movement. All of these efforts, one way or another, embraced the Cartesian masterplan: strict zoning laws and spatial compartmentalization created veritable Alphavilles of the body and mind. In response, the Situationists defended the urban mix, wanted to get beyond the rational city, strove to reassert daring, imagination and play in social life and urban culture. And crucial therein was the notion of 'constructed situations'.

Play, as well as politics, was fundamental to any Situationist situation. Play nourished politics, and political man was very much *Homo ludens*. The idea had been brilliantly expressed by the Dutch historian and medieval specialist Johan Huizinga, whose insights Debord had studied in the early 1950s and tried to make part of Situationist culture. 'The latent idealism of the author', Debord wrote of Huizinga in issue 20 of *Potlatch* (30 May 1955), 'doesn't devalue the basic contribution his work constitutes.' 'It is now a question', he added, 'of converting the rules of play from an arbitrary convention to a moral foundation.'[42] In *Homo ludens*, originally published in 1938, Huizinga reckoned that 'Man the

Player' deserved a rightful place in our nomenclature alongside *Homo sapiens* and *Homo faber* (man the maker).

One of the major characteristics of play, Huizinga said, was its *free* nature. Play was somehow about freedom, about stepping out of real life, entering a sphere of activity with its very own disposition. Therein lay play's strength. 'It adorns life', he wrote, 'amplifies it and is to that extent a necessity both for the individual – as a life function – and for society by reason of the meaning it contains, its significance, its expressive value.'[43] Combat and war, Huizinga believed, also had play elements, which sparked Debord's own ludic and combative passions. In the Middle Ages, flamboyant tournaments, jousting and duels involving quixotic knights with chivalric codes of honour were rituals redolent of the play-spirit.

> Fighting, as a cultural function, always presupposes limiting rules, and it requires, to a certain extent anyway, the recognition of its play-quality. We can only speak of war as a cultural function so long as it is waged within a sphere whose members regard each other as equals or antagonists with equal rights; in other words its cultural function depends on its play-quality.[44]

'Situations' were typically slippery and similarly playful Situationist inventions, as much metaphorical as material, with their own 'war game' rules and mentality. In a way, that's what gave them their power. Situations were meant to be fleeting happenings, moving representations, the 'sum of possibilities'. They'd be something lived, but also 'lived-beyond', full of possibilities. Debord and the Situationists wanted to 'construct' new situations, new life 'concretely and deliberately constructed by the collective organization of a unitary ambience and a game of events'. 'New beauty can only be a beauty of situation.' Situations would be practical and active, designed to transform context by adding to the context, assaulting or parodying context, especially one where the status quo prevailed.

What would emerge was a 'unitary ensemble of behaviour in time'.

Here time becomes ephemeral: every situation became a 'passageway' somewhere into an imminent present without a future. In fact, situations were, according to Debord's film of 1959, 'the passage of some people through a rather brief period of time'. 'The neighbourhood', announces a male voice-over, 'was made for the unfortunate dignity of the petite bourgeoisie, for respectable occupations and intellectual tourism. The sedentary population of the upper floors was sheltered from the influences of the street.'[45] Old documentary footage of Saint-Germain-des-Prés in the fog is shown; elsewhere, there are panoramic views of Les Halles, whose old market square overflows by day with people and vendors pushing little carts but becomes eerily melancholy at night and at dawn. Instead of just darkened screens, this time Debord's dialogue and images are interspersed with white screens. 'Everything being linked', said a voice,

> we needed to *change everything* by a unified struggle, or nothing. We needed to reconnect with the masses, but around us is sleep . . . our life is a voyage – in winter and in the night – we seek our passage . . . There was the fatigue and cold of morning in this well-travelled labyrinth, like an enigma that we had to resolve. It was a reality of illusions through which we had to discover the possible richness of reality.[46]

Situations tried to relay ambience, reunifying what had previously been sundered. They were group preoccupations reasserting texture and quality to place, glorifying free play. Members of si coined a few ingenious methods to prompt this cause. One was *dérive*, or drift, 'a mode of experimental behaviour linked to the condition of urban society'. *Dérive* was a continuous flow in which protagonists embarked upon a Surrealist trip, a dreamy trek though varied Parisian passageways, forever on foot, wandering for hours, usually at night, identifying subtle moods and nuances of neighbourhoods.

They'd map the city's substructure, and primitive walkie-talkies helped them to communicate with each other, sometimes miles apart. Through these real and imagined perambulations, Situationists became latter-day *flâneurs*, aimless urban strollers who weren't quite so aimless.

As they shifted in and out of public spaces, they were intent on accumulating rich qualitative data, grist to their 'psychogeographical' mill, documenting odours and tonalities of the cityscape, its unconscious rhythms and conscious melodies: ruined façades, foggy vistas of narrow, sepia-soaked streets, nettle-ridden paving stones, empty alleyways at 3 a.m., menace and mayhem, separation and continuity.[47] Commenting on the Situationists in 1983, Henri Lefebvre, the veteran Marxist philosopher and professor, said that *dérive* was

> more of a practice than a theory. It revealed the growing fragmentation of the city. In the course of its history, the city was once a powerful organic unity; for some time, however, that unity was becoming undone, was fragmenting, and the Situationists were recording examples of what we had all been talking about . . . We had a vision of a city that was more and more fragmented without its organic unity being completely shattered.[48]

Debord and the Situationists was a subject close to Henri Lefebvre's heart. 'One I care deeply about', he admitted. 'It touches me in some ways very intimately because I knew them very well. I was close friends with them. The friendship lasted from 1957 to 1961 or '62, which is to say about five years . . . In the end, it was a love story that ended very, very badly.'[49] Lefebvre was 30 years older than Debord, a prolific scholar and *bon vivant*, famous for popularizing Marx and Hegel, for books like *La Conscience Mystifiée* and *Dialectical Materialism*, as well as the path-breaking *Critique of Everyday Life*. Lefebvre's Marxism was unashamedly festive and rambunctious, prioritizing 'lived moments', irruptive acts of contestation: building occupations and street demos, free expressionist art and theatre, flying pickets, rent strikes and a general strike. Like the Situationists, for some of whom he was a mentor in the early 1960s at the University of Strasbourg, Lefebvre loved the idea of politics as festival. Rural festal traditions, he wrote in *Critique of Everyday Life*, 'tightened social links at the same time as they give free rein to all desires which have been pent up by collective discipline and necessities of work.' Festivals represent 'Dionysiac life . . . differing from everyday life only in the explosion of forces which had been slowly accumulating in and via everyday life itself.'[50]

The two men became acquainted through women. Like Debord, Lefebvre was a peculiar mix of Rabelaisian monk and Kierkegaardian seducer. Michèle Bernstein's childhood friend, Evelyne Chastel, was then Lefebvre's girlfriend, despite the considerable age gap. One day, the couples bumped into each other on a Parisian street, not long after Lefebvre had quit the French Communist Party. (For thirty years, he'd feuded with its Stalinist hacks.) Debord was very happy finally to meet the theorist whose work he'd read and admired. 'I remember marvellous moments with Guy', Lefebvre recalled in *Le Temps des méprises* (Times of Contempt) 'warm friendship, free of all mistrust and ambition.'

He and Debord drank together and often talked all night, engaging in 'more than communication', Lefebvre remembered, 'a communion – which remains an extremely vivid memory'. Back then, Lefebvre was probably Debord's only *living* influence, even though Debord was never a Lefebvre student; meanwhile, the young man with glasses, the brains of the Situationists, charmed the older academic. They shared ideas and shaped each other's visions of Marxism, praxis and the city. 'I remember very sharp, pointed discussions', Lefebvre said, 'when Guy said that urbanism was becoming an ideology. He was absolutely right, from the moment that there was an official doctrine of urbanism.'

They read Malcolm Lowry's *Under the Volcano* together, supping not a few mescals themselves, exploring revolutionary politics and theory, and Debord even helped to organize Lefebvre's teaching schedule. Debord and Bernstein sojourned at Lefebvre's rambling summerhouse in the Pyrenean foothills at Navarrenx. (Bernstein famously freaked out on one muddy country *dérive*.) And through Lefebvre Debord met the young Belgian poet and free spirit Raoul Vaneigem, another avid Lefebvre reader who'd soon enter the Situ fray, bursting onto the scene with brilliant texts like *The Revolution of Everyday Life* and *The Book of Pleasures*.[51] Around this time, too, Lefebvre discovered Constant and other anarchist Provos in Amsterdam, who later came to Paris and discovered Debord and his crew. 'I went to Amsterdam to see what was going on', Lefebvre remembered.

> There were Provos elected to the city council in Amsterdam . . . Then, after that, it all fell apart. All this was part and parcel of the same thing. And after 1960 there was the great movement in urbanization. The Situationists abandoned the theory of Unitary Urbanism, since Unitary Urbanism only had precise meaning for historic cities, like Amsterdam, that had to be renewed, transformed. But from that moment the historic city exploded peripherally, into suburbs, like what happened in Paris and all sorts of places . . . And then I think even the *dérive*, the *dérive* experiments were little by little abandoned. I'm not sure how this happened, because that was the moment I broke with them.[52]

2

The Café of Lost Youth

The storms of youth precede brilliant days . . .

Comte de Lautréamont, *Poésies*

Those close to Guy Debord say that he was charming, fearsomely erudite and difficult, likely to break off friendships as quickly as he established them. 'It is better to change friends than ideas', he liked to practice and preach. He was a man who didn't compromise for anyone, himself included. He was radical like Lautréamont, and modern like Cravan; but ancient like Omar Khayyám and Li Po, two of his favorite poets. Omar Khayyám's *Rubáiyát*, like the four-line stanzas of the Tang poet Li Po, express central Debordian motifs, inspiring motifs he'd never renounce: a life of drink and wandering, the desire for freedom and pleasure, the finite nature of time and the uncertainty of the future. 'Today', Omar Khayyám wrote,

tomorrow is not within your reach
To think of it is only morbid:
If the heart is awake, do not waste this moment –
There is no proof of life's continuance.

In the extremity of desire I put my lip to the pot's
To seek the elixir of life:
It puts its lip on mine and murmured,
'Enjoy the wine, you'll not be here again.'

'Every night', wrote Li Po,

> I come back from the river bank, drunk
> I have an unpaid bill
> in every tavern.
> Well, who lives to be seventy
> Anyway?

'Debord had one of the sharpest minds I have ever encountered',
recalled Ralph Rumney in his autobiography, *The Consul*. 'First,
there was his voice, then his language, which was always elegant.
Guy had charisma, genius, but also had a kind of hold, a kind of
power, over whatever was going on around him.' He was 'magic,
but malicious, too, when he wanted to be. Always delightful and
then, from one day to the next, bang, he would shut the door in
your face.'[1] Those who surrounded Debord in the 1950s and '60s
were young and fanatical, talked about philosophy, art, film,
politics, and drank a lot, usually in cheap cafés and bars, sometimes in the radical milieu of the Latin Quarter, at other times
with the proletariat of the Marais.

Chez Moineau's at 22 rue du Four was an infamous Debordian
hole-in-the-wall where he hung out and drank with Rumney and
others. Close to the fashionable existentialist world of Café de
Flore and Les Deux Magots, it was a universe away in terms of
clientele. Under Debord's poor cloak was an already legendary
drinker. He was a regular at Chez Moineau, whose mainstay wasn't
bourgeois highbrow types like Sartre and de Beauvoir, but hoods
and gangsters, prostitutes and pimps, dropouts and runaways,
petty criminals and alcoholics, latter-day accomplices of François
Villon, misfit characters from the pages of Céline, Mac Orlan
and Genet. This *demi-monde* was his perpetual source of play
and adventure. 'Paris then was never asleep in its entirety, and
permitted you to debauch and to change neighbourhoods three

times each night. Its inhabitants hadn't yet been driven away and dispersed.'[2] In Paris,

> there remained a people who had ten times barricaded its streets and routed its kings. It was a people who didn't give themselves to images . . . The houses were not deserted in the centre, nor resold to spectators . . . The modern commodity still hadn't come to show us what it could do to a street. Nobody, because of urban planners, was obliged to go to sleep far away. You still hadn't seen, by the fault of government, the sky darken and the good times disappear, and the false fog of pollution permanently covering the circulation of things in the valley of desolation.[3]

The city still had time for 'unmanageable riff-raff ', for 'the salt of the earth', for 'people quite sincerely ready to set the world on fire so that it had more brilliance'.[4] In fact, the city was so beautiful that many people preferred to be poor there, rather than rich somewhere else; they preferred, like Debord, to lead an 'openly independent life', finding themselves at home in 'the most ill-famed company'.

In his Lettrist memoir *The Tribe*, Jean-Michel Mension remembers drinking *vin ordinaire* with Debord on the terrace outside the Mabillon café on the boulevard Saint-Germain. Debord had money, Mension said: 'he got living expenses from his family, because officially he was a student'. It was Mension's eighteenth birthday and he ended up dead drunk. 'That was the beginning of our friendship; we sealed it that day, so to speak. After that we went drinking together every day for several months. We would go drinking, just the two of us, Guy and his bottle and I with mine. He was usually the one to pay.'

They'd often go to cour de Rohan, a little courtyard off rue de l'Ancienne-Comédie, 'and settle down in the passageway – there are some steps there, and we would sit on the bottom step, holding forth. In other words, we would set the whole world to rights while polishing off a litre or perhaps two litres of wine. That was our aperitif, in a manner of speaking, before we went over to Moineau's.'[5] Debord was highly cultivated, had a lot of finesse, and, of course, was enormously well read. 'Guy had obviously read and studied Marx', Mension recalled, 'and he was trying to transcend Marx; the Marxist starting point in Debord is plain to see'.[6] He 'dealt with Marxism at length, he read it all, but in my time we never discussed Marx'. 'This was really the first time I had met a guy who gave me the feeling he was beginning to answer the questions I had been asking myself about a world that was not my world, either East or West, either the Stalinist side or the bourgeois side. And an answer had to be found.'[7]

He was 'on a quest', Mension said, always 'goal-oriented', having big ideas about how to destroy society, on paper and in practice. And he was as methodical about drinking as he was about thought: 'Guy always drank in an amazing way, taking little sips from morning till night. You didn't notice him drinking.' You never saw him drunk. 'I remember a few occasions when he got close, but he never took that fatal glass that would have put him over the edge.'[8] At Moineau's, alcohol flowed in 'a perpetual stream', and everybody was at it. Sometimes they drank the place dry. Most of the clientele were flat broke, or near it; and the *patronne*, Madame Moineau herself, wasn't much better off. By all accounts, she was a *Bretonne* and used to wear an old blue apron, looking more like a cleaning lady than a café owner. She was there every day and night, cooked and scrubbed floors 'and loved us all like a grandmother'. 'She was a saint, she was our mother during that period.' In the 1950s Moineau's was a little zone of free play, a home away from home, where young people supped, sang, played chess, talked books and fell in and out of love. 'No one really had any secrets from anyone else.'[9]

Debord adored Paris: it was his stomping ground, his laboratory. He bore the burden of its travails, taking them very personally, very politically. He was what the Italian Marxist Antonio Gramsci would have labelled an 'organic intellectual': he belonged to a place and to a people, and he felt their 'elemental passions'. And yet, more and more, this belonging and Debord's kind were being threatened, were being displaced, torn down and torn apart, as neighbourhoods began to get readjusted and reordered. Henri Lefebvre, who didn't live far away from Debord and Michèle Bernstein, remembered their inhabiting 'a kind of studio on rue Saint Martin, in a dark room, no lights at all'. It was 'a miserable place, but at the same time a place where there was a great deal of strength and radiance in the thinking and the research'.[10] Nobody knew how Debord got by. He had no job, didn't want a job, opting instead to reside in a rich and happy poverty, a privilege long gone for most big city dwellers.

Debord and Bernstein lived together at 180 rue Saint Martin in the 3rd *arrondissement* in an apartment of barely 30 square metres, with a toilet outside along the corridor, which Michèle acquired with her father's aid. They'd met in 1952 and married two years later, a marriage that was to last eight years. Bernstein gave her own artful glimpse of their libertine nocturnal life in 1960 in a thinly disguised novel, *Tous les chevaux du roi* ('All the King's Horses'). The protagonists Gilles and Geneviève are dead ringers for Guy and Michèle. 'If Gilles no longer loved the same young women as me', the narrator Geneviève muses to herself, 'that introduced an element of separation between us'.[11] 'I know Gilles' taste for spending whole nights wandering', she says elsewhere,

> when an open café becomes a precious port of call in streets where night-birds aren't abundant. After 2 a.m., the rue Mouffetard is empty. You need to go back up to the Panthéon to find a bar, rue Cujas. The next stop is near to the Sénat, then rue du Bac, if you have the good taste to avoid what we still call the neighborhood . . . And, at daybreak, to Les Halles, which is a ritual.[12]

Gilles, we hear, seemed to be at once too young and too old for these times. 'What do you work as?' somebody asks him. 'How do you occupy your time?' 'With reification', answers Gilles. 'That's very serious work, I imagine, with a lot of thick books and a lot of papers on a grand table', quips his interlocutor. 'No', says Gilles. 'I wander, principally I wander.'[13]

Back in Gilles's and Geneviève's day, Parisian rents were bearable; cheap thrills were still to be had, cold-water affordability was possible. With Michèle, Debord lived only a stone's throw away from Les Halles, the old fruit and vegetable market halls, destined to be demolished in 1971 to make way for the rapid commuter train. (The Centre Pompidou, completed six years later, would seal the neighbourhood's fate.) Before that, Les Halles had been a sprawling, delirious, humdrum world, intensely alive, bawdy and beautiful, an urban paradise for Debord. When Baudelaire wrote in *Le Voyage* 'To plunge into the abyss . . . And find in depths of the unknown the new', it might have been the old Les Halles he was describing. In *To the End of the World* (1956), Blaise Cendrars, a nomadic scribe and a Foreign Legion veteran with only one arm, takes us on a cascading, roller-coaster ride through Debord's old seedy neighbourhood:

> From the *Halles* rose a rancid, fermented exhalation of rotting bananas and sick flowers, a mouldy sewer-smell that invaded the room, a mustiness that mingled with the window-rattling of motors starting off, the sounds of heavy lorries that shook the house to its foundations, the hooters that blew one atop the other in a skyscraper of sound, a dysentery of thunder, the shouts of the workmen unloading, jawing at each other as they manoeuvred their barrows; it mingled as well with the shifting shadows and lights that wandered over the ceiling. It was inhabited by polite little people, eccentric, pleasure-loving, rakish, gluttonous, respecting nothing, refined to their fingertips, though not very well-dressed, behaving every day as if it were a holiday and considering unemployment a blessing.[14]

Debord's vagabond peregrinations around Paris followed the well-trodden path staked out long ago by the *voyou* (hoodlum) of all *voyous*, François Villon, the medieval poet and *mauvais garçon*. Villon wrote intensely personal and lyrical poetry, as in his masterpiece *The Testament* (1462), as well as some wonderfully ribald verses in slang that Debord fondly cites in his books. Villon often used the argot of the Coquillards, an organized criminal underworld with their own secret language, a tongue no outsider could decipher. The canonical French poet had loose Coquillard connections; his friend Régnier de Montigny, petty hood, cop beater and kleptomaniac, a prototypical Jean Genet character, was a Coquillard, as was Colin de Cayeux, one of Villon's companions in the notorious College of Navarre robbery, when one Christmas night they climbed over a high wall, picked the lock of a safe, and made off with the school's coffers. 'We had several points of resemblance', Debord claimed in *Panégyrique*,

> with those other devotees of the dangerous life who had spent their time, exactly five hundred years before us, in the same city and on the same side of the river . . . there had been that "noble man" among my friends who was the complete equal of Régnier de Montigny, as well as many other rebels destined for bad ends; and there were the pleasures and splendour of those lost young hoodlum girls who kept us such good company in our dives and could not have been that different from the girls the others had known under the names of Marion l'Idole or Catherine, Biétrix and Bellet.

Throughout the 1950s and '60s, Debord and his band of coquillards inhabited their own little patch, their own 'zone of perdition', where as 'Fair children' they followed Villon warning from *The Testament*:

The central 'halle' of the market at Les Halles, 1950.

Be careful not to lose
the finest flower in your hat;
you, my clerks, whose fingers are like glue,
if you must take to robbing
or to swindling, save your skins!
For when he tried these things
(thinking an appeal would work)
Colin de Cayeux lost his.[15]

Villon preached in his 'poems in slang':

Keep changing outfits and ducking into churches;
take off, make sure your
clothes don't trip you up.
To show the others
they strung up Montigny;
he babbled to the crowd a while,
and then the hangman snapped his neck.

And:

> Prince of jerks who stick around,
> hit the open road, move on,
> and always keep your eyes peeled
> for the hangman's filthy paws.[16]

Graced with a few sous in his pocket, Debord conquered the city between midnight and three in the morning, glimpsing what the novelist Pierre Mac Orlan, another Debord favourite, called the *fantastique social*. This was a sensibility neither supernatural nor paranormal, but profoundly everyday, reserved for back streets and damaged people, for twilight nooks and crannies, for shadowy bars and taverns, frequently animated by liquor and invariably dramatized by departure, departures never made. One glimpsed the urban fantastic for a thrilling instant, tapped its hidden recesses by tapping the idiosyncrasies of the imagination. 'To give an explanation to the fantastic', Mac Orlan said in the 1920s, 'is a difficult thing. All explanations of the fantastic are, besides, arbitrary. The fantastic, like adventure, only exists in the imagination of those who search for it. One reaches, by chance, the goal of adventure. Try as one does to penetrate its aura, the mysterious elements that populate it disappear.'[17]

But by the mid-1970s this pungent underworld of shady, fantastical adventure was nearly gone, destroyed in the name of economic progress and sound planning. 'The assassination of Paris' became the pithy thesis of Louis Chevalier's damning 1977 autopsy on Gallic urbicide, which denounced those 'polytechnicians' – elite bureaucrats educated at France's *grandes écoles* – who'd systematically orchestrated the deadly *coup de grâce*. Chevalier took his native city to heart, agonized over its woes, and Debord acknowledged a strange affinity with the conservative scholar.

It could almost be believed, despite the innumerable earlier testimonies of history and the arts, that I was the only person to have loved Paris; because, first of all, I saw no one else react to this question in the repugnant 'seventies'. But subsequently I learned that Louis Chevalier, its old historian, had published then, without too much being said about it, *The Assassination of Paris*. So we could count at least two righteous people in the city at that time.[18]

Debord, like Chevalier, hated Le Corbusier and all he stood for. In 1925 the Swiss-cum-Parisian planner had proposed his 'Voisin Plan', a vision for a modern Paris that would update Haussmann's boulevards, replacing them with a gigantic expressway grid pattern, achieving in central Paris what Robert Moses hadn't achieved in downtown Manhattan. Sixteen enormous skyscrapers would likewise sprout up along the banks of the Seine, converting Paris into a thoroughly modernized radiant city, a real life Alphaville. The plan, of course, was a non-starter; yet the mentality persisted. The highways came, like the Right-Bank expressway in 1976, named the 'Georges-Pompidou Expressway' after the Republic's president, gouging out the old quays of the Seine. And the towers went up, as at Montparnasse, and at the westerly business node, La Défense, where Cartesian glass and steel towers created pseudo-public spaces of desolation and flatness. Close by, meanwhile, the 'new' city of Nanterre, 'whose boredom, hideousness, rawness, whose reinforced concrete condemned students to a kind of captivity and summed up all they detest'. 'The young now spit on Paris, Paris that had for centuries been their paradise, the city to which they flocked, convinced they would find there all they dreamed of – pleasure, love, success, glory.'[19]

Paris had been victim of a 'Grande Bouffe', a greedy feast of rape and pillage, undertaken by technocrats in cahoots with a new breed of business executives, more brazenly entrepreneurial than their forebears, frequently schooled in America. Together,

as an abundance of dispossession.

Still from the film *The Society of the Spectacle*.

they had reorganized Parisian space rationally, re-forged it in
their own crass class image. Paris once stood for 'people from all
walks of life and all classes, people of all sorts, from high society,
from the middling sort, from no society at all'.[20] Now the new
consumerist Paris, the Paris of the spectacle, 'is a closed universe,
disinfected, deodorized, devoid of the unexpected, without surprises,
with nothing shocking, a well-protected universe'.[21]

Those 'bards of conditioning', Debord knew, had assassinated
Paris, making a killing in the process. The city had died in his
arms, in her prime, from a 'fatal illness'. It was 'carrying off all the
major cities, and this illness is itself only one of the numerous
symptoms of the material decadence of a society. But Paris had
more to lose than any other. It was a great fortune to have been
young in this town when, for the last time, she shone with a fire
so intense.'[22] Paris's centre has been colonized by the well-heeled,
expelling the poor to the periphery, miles out in the *banlieue*. It was
an expulsion with nineteenth-century roots, begun in earnest in

the 1850s when the Prefect of the Seine, Baron Georges Haussmann, Louis-Napoleon's 'demolition artist', blasted and brutally hacked open medieval Paris, wiping out dirty working-class neighbourhoods. This gerrymandering set a historical precedent, contested only twice since, whereby low-income dwellers found themselves shoved out and priced off the land, scattered around the farthest reaches of the city, and deprived of their urbanity, of their 'right to the city'.

Bulldozers and the wrecker's ball never actually made it to the Latin Quarter, not since Haussmann's day; but the tourist cafés, wine bars and restaurants, as well as antique shops and chic boutiques, have now just as effectively seen off this neighbourhood. Unsurprisingly, Moineau's is a distant memory. Dodging traffic across the boulevard Saint-Germain and journeying on to rue du Four offers little novelty for the present-day wanderer, for any intrepid urbanist intent on serendipity. This is where Debord found and lost his youth, where 'we no more than other men could stay sober on this watch'. But it's a watch that has now undergone solid *embourgeoisement*. On the boulevard Saint-Michel, the Gibert-Jeune bookstore still stocks Debord's books, now canonized by Editions Gallimard. They still sell, of course, and find avid readers, many of them learning Debordian thought by rote for their media or cultural studies assignments. In these rarefied circles, the 'society of the spectacle' becomes an academic catchphrase, not a revolutionary byword.

Like Debord, Chevalier saw the destruction of Les Halles' old market halls as *the* violation of Paris, its real sacking, its real assassination. 'With Les Halles gone, Paris is gone.' The 27 February 1969 proved Les Halles' last waltz, its long-dreaded last night, when Parisians must have felt the same pain that New Yorkers had felt when old Penn Station was torn down three years earlier. There was hardly anyone to contemplate the scene, Chevalier recalled, save 'a few nocturnal creatures, a few nostalgia seekers, a few poets, a few *clochards*'.[23] Soon everybody was ousted, a crater hacked out, and the 'hateful' Centre Pompidou crushed everything under a mountain of dust. Renzo Piano's and Richard Rogers's national centre of arts and culture, with its 'frightful jumble of pipes and conduits and ducts', dubbed 'the gas works', filled the hole but only added to the void. 'It is blue', Chevalier quipped, 'yet Paris is grey.' Nearby, a subterranean cave called The Forum, 'a deep, fetid underground', concentrating all the high-class merchandise that Paris had to show off, rubbed salt into the wounds. If the Sacré-Coeur trampled over the legacy of the Communards, Pompidou did likewise over *les soixante-huitards*. (Debord abhorred the Centre Pompidou. In a twist of fate, the complex held a big Situ retrospective in 1989, inviting Debord to a private viewing. He refused.)

From the late 1950s onwards, urban planners everywhere ruthlessly began to assault older neighbourhoods, chopping them up into new functional units, purposely mobilizing renewal, bulldozing frayed but healthy quarters. Cities were marching to Le Corbusier's infamous battle cry: *supprimer la rue!* ('eliminate the street'). Streets, said Corbusier, symbolized disorder and disharmony; they were everything that was bad about urbanism, everything that belied a city out of sync with the machine age. They needed 'readjusting', he said. The city needed a new plan, with streets in the sky. Sidewalks down below, cafés like Moineau's, pavement life like Les Halles, were all 'fungi' that required weeding; flowers – or 'forests of pillars' – needed replanting in their stead.

In a typically racy polemic, 'Les Gratte-Ciel par la Racine' (skyscrapers by the root), published in *Potlatch* of 20 July 1955, Debord debunked Le Corbusier's 'radiant' nostrums. It was 'life definitely divided in enclosed blocks, in monitored societies; the end of any chance of insurrection and of encounter; automatic resignation'.[24] Streets full of people were henceforth incompatible with highways full of cars. 'But, in our eyes, pedestrian voyages are not monotonous or sad; the social laws aren't fixed in stone; the habits that we need to attack head-on have to make room for the incessant renewal of wonders; and the main comfort that we wish to be eliminated are ideas of order, and the flies who propagate them.' Le Corbusier was 'a particularly repugnant man, clearly more cop than anything else.'[25]

Debord's chief grumble was that of *separation*. The preeminence of order meant compartmentalization – of activity and people – in the name of efficiency. Everything had its place, its function: work here, residence there, leisure somewhere else. Spaces got hacked up and simplified, people got decanted, experience flattened. Separation meant the compartmentalization of consciousness, an inability for people to understand the totality of their lives. Separation in the city and in activity spelt separation in the mind, alienation, false consciousness, a retreat into contemplation. In 1961 Debord released his film *Critique of Separation*. 'Our epoch accumulates power and has rational dreams', a voice enunciates, in characteristic monotone.

> But no one recognizes these powers as their own. There is no access into adulthood: only the possible transformation, one day, of this long anxiety into a measured sleep. It is because no one ceases to be held in guardianship. The question of note isn't that people live more or less poorly; but always that the rules of their life escapes them.[26]

Then a subtitle flashes up, urging another intent: 'To give each person the social space essential for the expression of life.'[27]

In *Critique of Separation*, Debord's voice-over said: 'we have invented nothing. We adapt ourselves, with a few subtle differences, to a network of possible directions. We grow accustomed to it, it seems . . . In returning from an enterprise, everyone had less heart than when they had set out. Little dears, adventure is dead.'[28] As the film opens out onto a panoramic view of central Paris, he warned: 'As long as we are unable to make our own history, to freely create situations, the effort toward unity introduces other separations. The search for unified activity leads to the constitution of new specializations.'[29]

False unity meant a new kind of fragmentation. *Dérive* sought to reveal the idiocy of separation, trying to stitch together – by highlighting the gaping holes – what was spatially rent. *Dérive* paved the way for a more profound urban and spatial impulse: 'unitary urbanism', a central item in the Situationist lexicon and in Debord's thought. Unitary urbanism was a 'living critique'. It would battle against planners, efficiency experts and technocrats, those who sat in fancy offices high above everyone; it would work against market-driven cities, against developers for whom cities are merely merchandise. The unitary city would be disruptive and playful, reuniting physical and social separations. It would emphasize forgotten and beleaguered nooks and crannies, mysterious corners, quiet squares, teeming neighbourhoods, pavements brimming with strollers and old-timers with berets sitting on park benches.

In *Naked City* (1958), Debord and Asger Jorn deliberately cut up a map of Paris and rearranged the bits into a thrilling Dadaist collage. This kind of map gave all power to subjectivity, was 'psycho-geographical', and expressed insubordination and chance rather than certainty. Few works of art, Debord said, could rival the beauty of a Paris Metro map, especially for foot passengers! He recalled how a friend once wandered through the Harz region of Germany blindly following directions of a map of London. These antics were 'obviously only a mediocre beginning in comparison to the complete construction of architecture and urbanism that will someday be within the power of everyone'. Such would involve a 'revolution in everyday life'. (In a taped talk presented by an ever-elusive Debord at a 1961 Paris conference on Everyday Life, convened by Henri Lefebvre, he put his radical credentials firmly on the table, if not in person: 'The revolutionary transformation of everyday life isn't reserved to a vague future. It is immediately placed before us by the development of capitalism and its insupportable demands, the alternative being

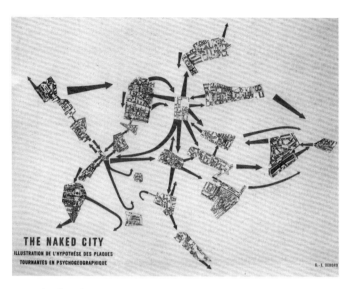

THE NAKED CITY
ILLUSTRATION DE L'HYPOTHÈSE DES PLAQUES
TOURNANTES EN PSYCHOGÉOGRAPHIQUE

G.-E. DEBORD

Guy Debord's and Asger Jorn's *Naked City*.

the reinforcement of modern slavery. This transformation will mark
the end of all unilateral artistic expression stocked under the form of
commodities, at the same time as the end of all specialized politics.')[30]
   This revolutionary mantra has its radical roots in the youthful
Karl Marx of 1844. When Marx drafted his *Economic and Philosophical
Manuscripts of 1844* in Paris he wasn't much younger than Debord,
and was just as idealistic. The manuscripts were unpublished in
Marx's day, only resurfacing in the 1930s and translated into French
as the country underwent its inter-war Hegel renaissance. Henri
Lefebvre's *Dialectical Materialism* (1939) became the chief conduit of
this Hegelian Marxism in France, and Debord had tuned in. He'd also
read Hegel and the philosopher who'd first put Hegel 'right side up',
Ludwig Feuerbach. Debord devoured Hegel's oeuvre in his younger
days and that close reading bore fruit with *The Society of the Spectacle*,
which is full of Hegelian motifs. Debord sat in on lectures given by
the great Hegel scholar Jean Hyppolite; and just before the publica-

tion of that book in 1967, he was all set to help the old professor out with a lecture at the Collège de France until Hyppolite had a change of heart and asked someone else.

Debord had likewise studied the Hegelian Marx at the source, and most citations that he uses tend to derive from the early Marx, particularly the *Economic and Philosophical Manuscripts*. There, Marx tried to affirm the primacy of 'free conscious activity' in the 'species-character' of human beings. He said that humans are endowed with 'vital powers', 'capacities' and 'drives', and are not merely contemplative, one-sided beings.[31] We come to know ourselves, Marx said, not by turning inward contemplatively, but by reaching out and feeling, seeing and comprehending the external world around us, the world outside our mind. Through practice, humans refashion external nature at the same time as they refashion their own internal nature. Humans are protean beings, desiring differentiated practice, needing meaningful and fulfilling activity. Cut this off, convert it into a dread zone of necessity, and our essential powers are henceforth alienated.

Debord and the Situationists deployed *détournement* to monkey-wrench accepted behaviour, to create light, to *disalienate*. *Détournement* helped fill things in, make life richer. Squatting, building and street occupations are classic examples of *détournement*, as are graffiti and 'free associative' expressionist art. All these actions would exaggerate, provoke and contest. They'd turn things around, lampoon, plagiarize and parody, deconstruct and reconstruct ambience, unleash revolutions inside one's head as well as out on the street with others. They'd force people to think and rethink what they once thought; often you'd not know whether to laugh or cry. Either way, *détournement* couldn't be ignored: it was an instrument of propaganda, an arousal of indignation, action that stimulated more action. It was 'negation and prelude', inspired by Lautréamont. Numerous *détournements* of buildings lay at the core of unitary urbanism.

A prime example was the idea of the Dutch Situationist, Constant, whose prototypical city, New Babylon, intentionally reversed the Protestant tradition's association of Babylon with evil and whoring: 'Babylon the great, mother of whores and of earth's abominations', said the Book of Revelation (16–18). For Constant and Debord, the accursed city of Satan, the great whore Babylon – where a fear of fornication and impurity becomes bound up with a fear of the city – suddenly symbolized the good city of the future. Debord had coined the name one winter's night back in 1959, when he enthusiastically greeted Constant's preliminary drawing-board visions. Constant was taken by the idea of 'Dériville' until Debord proposed 'New Babylon'.[32] (The label stuck, even as their friendship waned.) Constant strove to model *dérive* by constructing more redolent passageways, shocking landscapes, superimposing routes and spaces onto each other, sometimes using existing cityscapes, at other times completely new cities. He conceived of urban environments brimming with texture, tone and topographic fantasy.

Some of Constant's plans are exhilarating, brightly coloured deconstructed landscapes and Plexiglas models of futuristic cities; a few actually look like giant aircraft hangars and half-finished shopping malls, massive construction sites with steel scaffolding gaping; others are sublime Piranesian labyrinths.[33] In their own inimitable way, these are raw attempts to 'concretize' unitary urbanism, to make Marx's normative Good Life, in which 'the free development of each is a condition for the free development of all', the means as well as the end. In New Babylon, all useful yet repetitive activity underwent automation; and technology, mobilized at the mass level, would release people from the daily drudge of necessity, guaranteeing a healthy dose of free time. There'd be big institutional transformations, too, like collective ownership of land and the means of production, together with the rationalization of the manufacturing of consumer goods, making scarcity old hat. Constant's city, like unitary urbanism itself – like *détournement* and *dérive* – revealed the lie of urbanism, *détourne*d for the sake of dis-alienation: 'we need to defend ourselves at all moments from the poetry of the bards of conditioning – to reverse their rhythms.'[34]

Debord cherished Paris musty and worn, caked in dust, like a well-thumbed rare book collection that still found faithful readers. He had a prodigious knowledge of antiquity, of classical French masters, whom he could cite from memory and allegorize at whim. He was fascinated by the past, by the tradition of the dead genera-tions. But he was also an experimental thinker and political pro-gressive, once confessing, in *In Girum Imus Nocte et Consumimur Igni*, his haunting film, a desire to 'rebuild everything'. Released in 1978, a year after Louis Chevalier's monograph, *In Girum*'s mono-tone voiceover uttered: 'no longer an issue between conservation and change. We were ourselves, more than anybody, people of change, in a changing time. The owners of society were obliged, in order to sustain themselves, to change what was the inverse of ours.'[35] With its black and blank screens, the film expressed both Debord's preservationist ideals and his prefigurative impulses.

Debord was a man of change; he wanted to rebuild everything, but he also loved the past. He somehow wanted to go back to the future, wanted to reconstruct the best of the old world in the worst of the new. He was thus a man of the future as well as the past, someone who wanted to connect with the past only insofar as it was a springboard to a possible future. He wanted to bring into our modern age the epic features of former ages, and propel them into a world yet to be, a world still awaited. The incessant, eternally reoccurring, trajectory of life is precisely reflected in the motif: we go round and round in the night. Time flows, like the rivers flowing through *In Girum*, sometimes the Seine, other times the Yang-tze, always moving; every ending has a new beginning, an *à suivre*, everything begins again in a new guise at the end. 'All this gone forever', Debord said, citing staple Li Po, 'everything slips away at once, events and men – like the relentless flow of the

Yang-tse, which loses itself in the sea.' Paris is gone forever; there is no stepping back, no second act. The city had become an 'ungovernable wasteland',

> where new sufferings disguise themselves under the name of ancient pleasures; and where people are so afraid. They go round and round in the night and are consumed by fire. They wake up alarmed, and groping, search for life. Rumour has it that those who were expropriating it have, to top it all, mislaid it. So here is a civilization that is on fire, completely capsizing and sinking.[36]

In Girum Imus Nocte et Consumimur Igni would be Debord's last truly experimental cinematic undertaking; he'd never make the like again. In a way, he didn't have to: *In Girum* was his masterpiece, his *chef-d'œuvre cinématographique*, his epic voyage brought to the screen, his very own *Iliad* and *Divine Comedy*. It is a film about film – or, more accurately, about anti-film. It's also a Situationist poem on the art of war, a document about the passage of time, a metaphysical exploration of Debord's mind, to say nothing of his threnody on Paris. (The outspoken critic and novelist Philippe Sollers believes the film's dialogue, which is reprinted in Debord's *Œuvres ciné-matographiques complètes*, to be 'one of the finest books of the twentieth century'.)[37]

It is Debord's most autobiographical and metaphysical venture. We glimpse him at various ages, at 19, 25, and at 45. We spot Alice, too, and her friend Céleste, in a crypto-lesbian embrace. There are aerial views of Paris, panned panoramas of nocturnal Les Halles, café entrances and interiors, cellars and caves, pirates and Robin Hood, scenes of cannon fire from battleships, cavalry charges, troop formations, battlefields, Custer's last stand, the charge of the Light Brigade, all interspersed with snippets from Clausewitz and Sun Tzu. The tone throughout is sad and forlorn, like a romantic refrain, like Chateaubriand's *René*, like a magnificent and terrible peace, the true taste of the passage of time. The lyrics are poetic: 'Midway through the path of real life, we were surrounded by a sombre melancholy, expressed in so much sad and mocking lines, in the café of lost youth.'[38]

It was there where 'we lived as forlorn children, our adventures incomplete'. Who else, he asked, could understand the beauty of Paris apart from those who can remember its glory? Who else could know the hardships and the pleasures we knew in these places where everything has become so dire? Once, the trees weren't suffocated, the stars not extinguished by the progress of alienation. Liars have always been in power, he knew; but now economic development had given rulers the means to lie about everything. How could he not remember the charming hooligans and proud girls with whom he inhabited these dingy dives?

> Although despising all ideological illusions, and quite indifferent to what would later prove them right, these reprobates had not disdained to declare openly what was to follow. To finish off art, to announce in the midst of a cathedral that God was dead, to undertake to blow up the Eiffel Tower, such were little scandals indulged in sporadically by those whose way of life was permanently such a large scandal. They pondered on why some revolutions failed; and asked if the proletariat really exists, and, if this was the case, what it could be.[39]

You could feel the earth move, Debord said, and time burn with an intense heat. But somehow, he knew, the domain of time had to be traversed in order to reach the goal of opportunity. One had to discover how to live, in the days to follow, in a manner worthy of such a fine beginning.

'As for myself', Debord mused, 'I have never regretted anything I've done, and I admit that I am completely unable to imagine what else I could have done, being what I am.'[40] Our formula for overthrowing the world, he said, wasn't found in books: we found it in wandering in the night. It lasted for days; no day was like the previous day, and it never ended. It was a quest for an unholy Grail, with astonishing encounters, remarkable obstacles, grandiose betrayals, perilous enchantments. We caught a fleeting glimpse, he said, of the object of our quest; we couldn't live in the spurious light of the true because we possessed very strange powers of seduction.

> We hadn't aspired to subsidies for scientific research, nor to the praise of newspaper intellectuals. We carried fuel to where the fire was. It was in this matter that we definitely enlisted the Devil's party, that is to say, in this historical evil that leads the existing conditions to their destruction; through the 'bad side' that makes history by ruining all established satisfaction.[41]

The Situationists had met 'to enter into a conspiracy of limitless demands', seeing 'glimmers of light in the setting sun of Paris', finding themselves 'enraptured with a beauty that would be swept away and which would not return.' 'We will soon need to leave this city that was for us so free, but which is going to fall entirely into the hands of our enemies. Already, without recourse, they're applying their blind law, remaking everything in their likeness, that is to say, on the model of a sort of cemetery.'[42] Society has always rewarded mediocrity, always rewarded those who kowtow to its unfortunate laws. 'Yet I am, precisely at this time, the only person to have had some renown, clandestine and bad, and whom they haven't succeeded to get to appear on this stage of renunciation . . . I am long practised at living an obscure and elusive existence.' It is a *métier* in which nobody can ever get a doctorate; thus spoke our doctor of nothing, our 'Prince of Division'. And so the epoch that Debord loved, with its thrills and innocence, melted away forever.

3

It Never Said Anything Extreme

When it rains, when there are false clouds over Paris, don't forget that
it's the government's fault. Alienated industrial production makes it
rain. Revolution brings fine weather.

Guy Debord, *La Planète malade*

Unlike a lot of other theorists, Guy Debord never wrote too much,
never said more than was necessary, never made a career out of
critique. His oeuvre is relatively modest, and each work rarely
exceeds 100 pages. 'Writing should remain a rare thing', he advised
in *Panégyrique*, 'since one must have drunk for a long time before
finding excellence.' When he did put pen to paper he did so with
beautiful economy, without affectation or fatigue. *The Society of the
Spectacle* endures as his masterpiece, his best-known text. It's a
wonderful little book, a brilliant prose poem. Debord saw the book
as an act of *demystification*, even as *de-sanctification*, as an exposé
of the modern form of the commodity, as an indictment of the
hypocrisy of our lives.

The text appeared in late 1967, published by Buchet/Chastel,
against a backdrop of an advancing post-war consumerism.
Capitalism was tapping the parts nobody – Marx included – could
have ever imagined: one-hundred-odd years on from *The Communist
Manifesto*, the system was more rampant and expansive than ever
before, in spite of its inherent crises. New market strategies, new
media, new acts of seduction, were colonizing leisure and consump-

tion as well as production, appropriating and re-appropriating space, capturing everybody's attention, pervading consciousness and consciences.

Everywhere commercial dictates intruded into everyday life, and critical scholars were trying to figure it all out. In France, Henri Lefebvre ruminated on the perplexing 'survival of capitalism' and on 'everyday life in the modern world'. In the USA, sociologists like David Riesman spotted 'lonely crowds', new types of low-grade alienation resulting from high-grade affluence; William H. Whyte chronicled the decaffeinated landscapes pioneered by smart 'organization men', those heads of bureaucracies and corporations who thrive on order and efficiency. Meanwhile, Marshall McLuhan harked that 'the medium is the message': it wasn't so much the content of the commodity that mattered as its form, not so much selling what you make as selling the sell. Capitalism was going virtual, de-coupling not only from real places, but from the very materiality of the commodity itself. As *The Society of the Spectacle*'s opening refrain, thesis 1, puts it: 'everything that was directly lived has moved away into a representation.'[1] The reality of things moved away into a spectacular reality of images, into a deceived gaze and stupefication.

After 1967 it was Debord himself who became the leading theorist and most ruthless antagonist of this new emergent phase of capitalism, something now economically more prodigious and ideologically more devious. The two flanks went hand in hand, rapidly becoming one flank; politics strove merely to manage the articulation. Now, the state, irrespective of ideological stripe, was itself subsumed within this system, and increasingly became a facilitator of spectacular capitalism, an executive committee managing the interests of a diverse (and sometimes destructive) bourgeoisie, forces and factions vying for spectacular growth and profits. Debord's treatise, subsequently translated into dozens of languages, attempted to delve into the belly of the fabulous beast, showing how commodity logistics penetrated new depths of modern life.

Meanwhile, he took Marx's analysis to new heights, the culmination of a fifteen-year meditation on the downfall of the state, begun in earnest in 1952 at Moineau's.

Its 221 short, strange, elegant theses, aphoristic in style and peppered with irony and a few Nietzschean inflections, were reminiscent of Marx's 'Theses on Feuerbach'. Their underlying content remained vividly (and quirkily) Marxian, uniting youthful humanism with mature political economy, a left-wing Hegel with a materialist Feuerbach, a bellicose Machiavelli with a utopian Karl Korsch, a military Clausewitz with a romantic Georg Lukacs. Debord gives us a compelling evocation of a world in which unity spelt division, essence appearance, truth falsity. It was, he said, a topsy-turvy world where everything and everybody partook in a perverse paradox. As the young Marx wryly pointed out in 1844,

> I am ugly, but I can buy for myself the most beautiful women. Therefore I am not ugly . . . I, in my character as an individual am lame, but money furnishes me with twenty-four feet. Therefore I am not lame. I am bad, dishonest, unscrupulous, stupid; but money is honored, and therefore so is its possessor . . . money is the real mind of all things and how can its possessor be stupid?[2]

Debord wanted to *détourn* the reality of this non-reality, this world where ugliness signified beauty, dishonesty honesty, stupidity intelligence. He wanted to subject it to his own dialectical inversion, to his own spirit of negation. In the process, he wrote a unique work of political art, utterly without precedent or peer. It was radical critique and militant call-to-arms. Its theoretical exegesis sought to reveal the fetishism, to name the alienation; its immanent battle-cry wanted to stir the working class to organize and mobilize, to develop workers' councils and end their slumbering torpor.

Active human agency had to be summoned up to confront spectacular 'contemplation'. Those icons of a hyper-modern capitalism, semiotics everyone today knows instinctively – be it MTV or CNN, Microsoft or News International, McDonald's' golden arches or Nike's swoosh – cast a soporific haze over life. People needed to shake up and wake up. For on show is an old enemy wrapped up in new clothing, and wearing a new mask. 'In the essential movement of the spectacle', Debord warned in thesis 35, paraphrasing Marx from *Capital*, 'which consists in possessing, in congealed state, all that existed in human activity in a fluid state . . . we recognize our old enemy, the commodity, who knows so well how to appear at first glance something trivial and obvious, while on the contrary is so complex and so full of metaphysical subtleties.' Thus, the metaphysical subtleties and theological niceties of the commodity required puncturing, warranted demystification. *The Society of the Spectacle* had, Debord claimed in 1992, 'been written with the intention of harming the spectacular society.' 'It had', he reasoned, 'never said anything extreme'.[3]

Much like Marx's concept of the 'value-form' of the commodity, the 'spectacle-form' of the commodity was both historical and strategic. Spectacular society was the hyper-reified world of *separation*, 'separation achieved', Debord labelled it: workers separated from their activity, from their products of labour, from their fellow workers, even from themselves. Reification happens when something is denied, when something is taken away from a thinking subject, displaced into an object, into a thing external to the self, against the self; it forcibly sunders the mind from itself, from the activity of thinking. The more the commodity united and universalized the world, the greater the subjugation and fragmentation of workers' consciousness. At the beginning of *Capital*, Marx pointed out how wealth in nineteenth-century capitalism appears as 'an immense accumulation of commodities'. In thesis 1 of *The Society of the Spectacle*, Debord again paraphrased Marx: 'In societies where modern conditions of production prevail, all of life presents itself as an immense accumulation of spectacles.' This was 'a pseudo-world apart', today a life where specialized images, global satellite networks, and high-tech gadgetry and multimedia dominate and cohere as 'autonomous images'.

It's a world where, in our own lexicon, bytes reign over rights, corporate promotion over civic commotion. Such a world 'says nothing more than "that which appears is good, that which is good appears"' (12). 'The attitude it demands in principle is this passive acceptance which it had, in fact, already obtained by the manner of its appearance without reply, by the monopoly of appearance.' The spectacle is fundamentally tautological: it's 'the sun that never sets on the Empire of modern passivity' (13). It 'doesn't realize philosophy', but 'philosophizes reality' (19). It is 'the nightmare of a modern society imprisoned', a society that 'only expresses its ultimate desire to sleep'. And the spectacle 'is the guardian of this sleep' (21). It is the subjugation of real men and women to an economy of images, the true reflection of the production of things in the human mind. The spectacle 'is capital to such a degree that accumulation has become an image' (34).

In *Capital*'s opening chapter, Marx insisted that a commodity's physicality, its palpable 'thing' quality, bore little or no connection to the social relations that made it. As an 'it' we hear nothing about social relationships between workers and owners, between minimum wage toilers and rich bosses, between Third World peasants and Wall Street stockbrokers. In the realm of the latter, the former is occluded, silenced, rendered imperceptible to the senses. This masking effect is something Marx deemed 'fetishism'. He asks us to address our amnesia and shortsightedness. He asks us to probe the root of things, to expose bourgeois deceit and ideology, to get a more process and relational grip on reality, to shift our perspective. This task of change, Debord knew, was now more troublesome, for the fetishism is total, even more complex, simply because there doesn't appear to be a fetishism anymore. Now, spectacular images make us want to forget – indeed, insist that we *should* forget.

In the *Economic and Philosophical Manuscripts*, Marx said that a worker 'does not confirm himself in his work, but denies himself, feels miserable and not happy, does not develop free mental and physical energy, but mortifies his flesh and ruins his mind. Hence the worker feels himself only when he is not working; when he is working he does not feel himself. He is at home when he is not working, and not at home when he is working.'[4] Debord said that workers now no longer feel at home even when they're not working; they're no longer themselves at home, given that work and home, production and reproduction – the totality of daily life – has been subsumed, colonized and invaded by exchange value. 'The spectacle', he said in thesis 42, 'is the moment when the commodity has reached the *total occupation* of social life.'

In leisure time, workers became consumers, mere bearers of money; private life became the domain of the advertisement, of fashion, of convenience and processed food, of movie and pop stars and glamorous soap operas, of dreaming for what you already know is available, at a cost. The spectacle is, thesis 44 insisted, 'the permanent opium war'. Free time and work time congealed into 'spectacular time'. All boundaries between economic, political and private life have thereby dissolved. All the consumable time and space became raw material for new products, for new commodities. 'The spectacle is the other side of money: it is the general abstract equivalent of all commodities' (49).

Marx's 'estranged labour' was now generalized into 'estranged life'; a 'false consciousness of time', time turned into an abstraction, time abandoned. Spectacular time represented an eternal present, the denial of death. The spectacle, Debord said, marked capitalism's seizure and denigration of history and memory; it equally signalled the seizure and denigration of space, which, like time, must be organized, ordered and patrolled. Disorderly old streets threaten the spectacular status quo; maintaining order in the street culminates in the suppression of the street. 'Isolated individuals' had to be 'recaptured' and 'isolated together', collected into 'factories and halls of culture, tourist resorts and housing developments', environments 'expressly organized to serve this pseudo-community that follows the isolated individual right into the family cell' (172). 'Capitalist production had unified space.' It is, thesis 165 went on,

> no longer limited by external societies. This unification is at the same time a process of extensive and intensive *banalization*. The accumulation of commodities serially produced for the abstract space of the market, just as it had to break all regional and legal barriers, all corporative restrictions of the middle ages that maintained the *quality* of artisanal production, also had to destroy the autonomy and quality of places.

In the second volume of *Panégyrique*, a fascinating photomontage of Debord's whole life and work – truth in images, he called it, a sort of iconic ensemble – there is a reproduction of the original 1967 handwritten manuscript. Debord wrote everything longhand in small, careful cursive, using those ordinary squared exercise books so common in France. *The Society of the Spectacle*'s manuscript has a good bit of crossing out and correction, hinting uncertainty and indecision on the part of the creator; yet it also exhibits a neatness and precision. You sense this is the work of a perfectionist and craftsman, someone self-assured, a stylist who isn't riddled with self-doubt, who takes pride, as Debord did, in *not* correcting himself, on being happy with their first finished effort. We can get close to Debord, the artist, if we get close to his work and learn how to look between the lines. We can learn from looking at him, too.

In another shot from *Panégyrique*, volume II, there's Debord, the 30-something scribe, hunched over, gripping a pen and deliberating over a notepad, wearing glasses and a scarf and looking very brainy. His seriousness doesn't seem feigned. We can imagine him to be a man who didn't smile often, despite having a dry wit. He didn't like to think of himself as an 'intellectual', we know; still, his mind operated almost intuitively at the intellectual level, through theory and abstraction. He was a classic man of ideas, who always romanticized his *other*, the practical man, somebody who imbibed the world corporeally and sensually. The caption underneath this photo, from Philippe de Commynes' *Mémoires*, reads 'by which one work will you be able to know the grandeur of the prince who speaks to you, and also to your understanding?'[5] *The Society of the Spectacle* provides the unequivocal answer.

Each thesis is itself as a *situation*, as a poetic punctuation. Its surrealist undertow conjures up the realm of dream, releases unconscious yearning and political sublimation. At the same time, Debord's insights are brutally realistic, wide-awake descriptions of what is and projections of what might be. For the first time, Marxist social theory is expressed as lyric poetry. Its tone reincarnates Lautréamont's *Poésies*, his style of negation, letting us glimpse the veritable meeting of the commodity and the sewing machine on a dissection table. Debord was rightly proud of *The Society of the Spectacle*, and was glad it became a modern French classic. 'I flatter myself', he commented in his 1979 preface to the fourth Italian edition,

> to be a very rare contemporary example of someone who has written without being immediately refuted by events, and I do not want to say refuted a hundred or a thousand times like the others, but not a single time. I have no doubt that the confirmation all my theses encounter ought to continue right until the end of the century, and even beyond.[6]

When the publisher Champ Libre, the brainchild of Debord's millionaire mogul friend-to-be Gérard Lebovici, offered to republish *The Society of the Spectacle* in 1971, Debord wanted 'nothing else for the cover of my book than a geographic map of the world in its entirety'. He said he wanted 'an atlas of the beginning of the twentieth century, a map whose colours represented the global development of commercial relations, where it was then realized, and where one expected its future course'.[7] The jacket of recent Gallimard editions possesses a brightly coloured *fin-de-siècle* globe, the colours representing an era of wide-reaching economic integration and internationalization, an epoch when, as Marx prophesied in the *Grundrisse*, capitalism really did 'annihilate space by time'.

Between 1880 and 1914 especially, the world market did come into its own; existing relations between nations and people were transformed, forever. It was a period when James Joyce, in *Ulysses*, heard 'the ruin of all space, shattered glass and toppling masonry', when erstwhile autonomous, self-sufficient absolute spaces became relativized, became incorporated into value relations and commodity exchange. This marked the real triumph of the world of things, the heavy artillery that battered down all Chinese walls. Debord knew it and wanted it on the front of his book. 'The root of the spectacle is in the terrain of the economy becoming abundant' (58). The society of the spectacle began everywhere in coercion, trickery and blood; and yet it promised happiness and prosperity.

Under the guise of separation, the spectacle nourished a 'unity of misery'. Behind the lure of choice were but different manifestations of alienation, bundled together into *intensive* and *extensive* forms of repression. Of the former variety, Debord called the spectacle 'concentrated'; the latter, 'diffuse'. Both deny and support each other. Together, they signify two rival and successive forms of spectacular power. The concentrated functioned through cult of personality, through dictatorship and totalitarianism, through brute and crude force; the diffuse was more ideological, and represented 'the Americanization of the world', a process that simultaneously frightens and seduces countries where traditional forms of bourgeois democracy once prevailed. After all, it guarantees freedom and affluence, dishwashers and Big Macs. When the spectacle is concentrated, the greater part of society escaped it; when diffuse, a small part.

But the split in this totality
mutilates it to the point of making

Still from the film *The Society of the Spectacle*.

The concentrated spectacle, Debord said, in thesis 64, 'belongs essentially to bureaucratic capitalism, even though it may be imported as a technique of state power in more backward mixed economies, or in certain moments of crisis in advanced capitalism'. Bureaucratic dictatorship of the economy 'cannot leave in the exploited masses any notable margin of choice, since it had to choose everything itself'. It has to ensure a permanent violence. 'The imposed image of the good internalizes the totality of what officially exists, and usually concentrates itself in a single man who is the guarantor of its total cohesion'. All Chinese once had to learn Mao and became Mao; every Soviet had to learn Lenin and Stalin, and became each man. They were heroic images, absolute celebrities, and Debord hated them and all they stood for. Meanwhile, the diffuse spectacle 'accompanies the abundance of commodities, the unperturbed development of modern capitalism'. Mass consumption and commodities fill the frame and pollute the mind; different merchandise glistens in stores. The diffuse spectacle thrives off the *gadget*, the gimmick, the fad. It indulges in the commodity, in accumulation for accumulation's sake, production for production's sake. With the diffuse spectacle, commodity fetishism reaches 'moments of fervent exaltation' whose only goal is the goal of submission.

The spectacle, Debord said, is 'the epic poem' of capitalism trying to impose its will on everything and everybody. It's a struggle that cannot stop unless it is forced to. Only the revolutionary subject, collectively organized and tactically mobilized, can threaten this 'twilight world', can 'subject space to lived time' (178). Lived time meant 'the critique of human geography through which individuals and communities have to construct sites and events corresponding to the appropriation of, not just their labour, but of their total history' (178). This would necessitate a reconstructed urbanism in accordance with 'the power of workers' councils, of an *antistatist dictatorship of the proletariat*', the 'greatest revolutionary idea' ever (179). This reconstruction would prompt a real 'sense of place', a successfully *détourne*d urban environment, so bridging the dialectic between particularity and generality, between its rooted identity and its open borders. It would re-establish the autonomy of place, 'without reproducing an exclusive attachment to the soil, and by reclaiming the reality of the voyage and of life understood as a voyage in every sense' (178).

Negation would retain something positive; pessimism would keep hold of a grain of optimism: the re-articulation of history opened up the possibility for a new history. Debord's radical politics in the 1960s lamented past times and spaces while holding a bitter yearning for a better tomorrow. His critique bewailed what the spectacle had taken away, especially in his adolescent Paris, and rallied for what had yet to be achieved in the post-spectacular age. He knew that critical theory could only go so far here: it wasn't sufficient in itself. Praxis was necessary to weld thought to action, to launch radical war. Otherwise, the concept of spectacle would become itself another spectacle, a hollow rhetoric, defending, in the final analysis, the same spectacular order it sought to over-throw. 'To effectively destroy the society of the spectacle', he said in thesis 203, 'it is necessary for people to put into action a practical force.' 'Unified critique' must somehow meet 'unified praxis'.

The proof of the pudding is in the eating. Theory, Debord knew, cannot expect miracles from the working class. All the same, work-ers, students, artists, activists and malcontents must somehow join hands, coordinate organization and unleash militant spontaneity. Streets would become the stage and the stake in this two-pronged radicalism. It was there where most harm might be done to the spec-tacle. Streets become the staging for spectacular 'counter-spectacles', sites for the construction of new participatory situations, for 'real war', not 'war on paper'. The ink had hardly dried: Debord's theory became a practical force, gripping the masses on Paris's streets, barely six months after its publication. 'To be free in 1968', read one wall graffito then, 'is to participate'. In his *Mémoires* the seven-teenth-century *agent provocateur* Cardinal de Retz prophetically wrote 'One could truly say that what makes them different from all other forms of power is their ability, having reached a certain point, to do everything which they believe themselves capable.'

The Society of the Spectacle became si's book of theory and therapy, entering the fray when working-class grievances in France festered and practical agitation simmered. The year 1967 was the one before revolutionary fervour came to the boil. This was theory that explained the context – be it of politics, cities or global economics. It identified enemy minefields and plotted a radical North-west Passage, 'a geography of real life'. It dug out city trenches beneath the cobblestones. 'The si', Debord wrote in a 1979 preface to the fourth Italian edition,

> was at this time the extremist group that had done the most to
> bring back revolutionary contestation to modern society; and it

May 1968 poster: 'Down with Spectacular-Commodity Society!'.

was easy to see that this group, having imposed its victory on the terrain of critical theory, and having skillfully followed through on the terrain of practical agitation, was then drawing near the culminating point of its historical action. So it was a question of such a book being present in the troubles that were soon to come and that would pass it on after them to the vast subversive sequel that these troubles could not fail to open up . . . Those who really want to shake an established society must formulate a theory that fundamentally explains it, or which at least has the air of giving a satisfactory explanation of it.[8]

The Society of the Spectacle was written on the walls of Paris and other capital cities and provincial towns in 1968: 'POWER TO THE WORKERS' COUNCILS', 'DOWN WITH SPECTACULAR-COMMODITY SOCIETY', 'THE END OF UNIVERSITY'. Its refrains were daubed all over the modern high-rise environment at the University of Paris at

May 1968 poster: 'Abolish Class Society!'

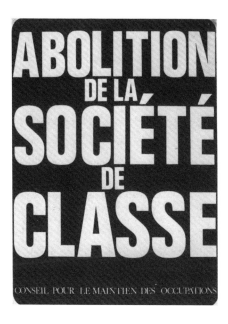

Nanterre, a classic scene of urban isolation and separation, a 'suburban Vietnam', where a peripheral 'new town' university coexisted with working-class slums and Arab and Portuguese shanty towns. The environment was sterile, sexually and socially repressive, and totalitarian. It was a microcosm of France's culture. This was the spirit of a society without any spirit. The same centralization, hierarchy and bureaucratic obsession persisting in the educational sector persisted in other aspects of the French state. Tough rules governed student dorms and freedom of movement, classes were overcrowded, resources stretched, professors were distant, student alienation rife. The right-wing Gaullist regime attempted to modernize the economy, adapting it to recent Common Market membership, and unemployment was growing, especially for younger workers.

At the University of Strasbourg, two years before, a handful of Situationists had intervened, Lefebvre's militant students and

Debord's friends. They'd tried to rile, denounce (including Lefebvre himself) and revolutionize students with an influential pamphlet, drafted by a Tunisian student, Mustapha Khayati, called 'On the Poverty of Student Life – Considered in its Economic, Political, Psychological, Sexual and Especially Intellectual Aspects, with a Modest Proposal for its Remedy'. They'd infiltrated the National Union of French Students (UNEF), accused students at Strasbourg and elsewhere of pandering to a society dominated by the commodity and the spectacle. Student poverty was a poverty of ideas, a poverty of guts. Students were really 'submissive children', labour-power in the making, without class-consciousness. They accepted the business and institutional roles for which the 'university-factory' prepared them, never questioning the system of production that alienated all activity, products, people and ideas. SI's text plainly struck a chord, and translated reprints extended its audience, notably to the USA, Britain and Italy. In Strasbourg, the document caused quite a scandal; a coterie of students refused to be integrated, refused co-optation. Critical awareness gathered steam over the next year, until 22 March 1968, when it blew a gasket in Paris, at Nanterre.

Members of SI, young communists, Trotskyists, anarchists and Maoists invaded the university's administration building, and began occupying it. The week before, the Committee of the Enragés and the Situationist International had been established. Its members put up posters and scribbled slogans on the walls of Nanterre and the Sorbonne: 'TAKE YOUR DESIRES FOR REALITY', 'NEVER WORK', 'BORE-DOM IS COUNTER-REVOLUTIONARY' 'TRADE UNIONS ARE BROTHELS', 'PROFESSORS, YOU MAKE US GROW OLD', 'IF YOU RUN INTO A COP, SMASH HIS FACE IN'. In early May, 'the 22 March Movement' met with UNEF at the Sorbonne in the Latin Quarter. The authorities tried to break up the meeting; instead they only unleashed its latent power. The *gendarmerie mobile* poured into the Sorbonne's courtyard and encircled its buildings. Several thousand students fought back, inside

Demonstration on the boulevard Saint Germain, 6 May 1968.

and outside, ripping up paving stones on the street. Skirmishes broke out elsewhere, spreading in the Latin Quarter, and flaring up at Châtelet and Les Halles. On 6–7 May a huge student demonstration took over the boulevard Saint Michel and thoroughfares near rue Gay-Lussac; protesters overturned cars, set them ablaze, dispatched Molotov cocktails, manned the barricades and stopped the flow of traffic. Cars no longer clogged up central Paris and the smog lifted. The revolution brought fine weather.[9]

On 13 May there was a one-day general strike; 'student-worker' solidarity suddenly looked possible, against the French Communist Party's (PCF) and general worker's union's (CGT) odds. Situationists and students *détourne*d the Sorbonne. On one revered fresco they emblazoned a witty cartoon caption: 'HUMANITY WILL ONLY BE HAPPY THE DAY THE LAST BUREAUCRAT IS HUNG BY THE GUTS OF THE LAST CAPITALIST'. Exams had been cancelled at the barricades; sociologists and psychologists became the new cops. Next day, workers at the Sud-Aviation plant in Nantes occupied their factory and locked out the bosses; meanwhile, Renault workers at Cléon, in Seine-Maritime, followed suit. Then the Nouvelles Messageries de la Presse Parisienne launched a wildcat action, halting newspaper distribution.

Workers' councils linked up with students' councils, becoming comrades in arms. The working class, at last, declared its unequivocal support for the student movement when rank and filers at Renault-Billancourt took over France's largest factory.

By 20 May strikes and occupations had become contagious. Nationwide, approximately 10 million workers downed tools and froze assembly lines. France seemed on the precipice of revolution; a festival of people was glimpsed. Alienation was cast off, momentarily; freedom was real; capitalized time abandoned. Without trains, cars, Metro and work, leisure time was reclaimed, time lived. Students and workers had seized the contingent situation, had acted spontaneously, had created new situations, and realized what no trade union or party could do, or wanted to do. And yet, as quickly as things erupted, they were almost as speedily violently and ideologically repressed, by the state and bourgeoisie. The optimistic promise, the beach beneath the paving stones, had dissipated, for now. The music was over. There was apparently no other side to break on through to.

The occupation of Paris was, and still is, seen throughout the world as an event of historical significance. Solidarity between workers had expressed itself; so had direct-action militancy; so had student internationalism, from the LSE to Berkeley, from Columbia to Nantes, from the Sorbonne to Barcelona; dissatisfaction had spread like wildfire. At the same time, *The Society of the Spectacle*'s demands were 'plastered in the factories of Milan as in the University of Coïmria. Its principal theses, from California to Calabria, from Scotland to Spain, from Belfast to Leningrad, infiltrate clandestinely or are proclaimed in open struggles.'[10] 'The Situationist International imposed itself in a moment of universal history as the thought *of the collapse of a world*; a collapse which has now begun before our eyes.'[11]

In old photos of the student occupations of the Sorbonne, Debord is visible in the thick of the action, lurking with intent. He was no student himself, of course; nor was he particularly youthful: in May 1968 Debord, the freelance revolutionary, was 36, older than a lot of junior professors, and almost twice the age of many student leaders (such as Daniel Cohn-Bendit). He must have seemed like an old man to many kids, somebody's dad drinking in the student union. Already his appearance had started to deteriorate. Surrounded by a large crowd of student activists, we can see him standing side on, without glasses, wearing a white jacket. His face is much puffier than a decade earlier; a boozer's physiognomy was rapidly becoming apparent. By comparison with other '68ers, who were mere political toddlers, he was a veteran *provocateur*.

Debord and other Situationist politicos were genius agitators and organizers, and their presence was felt, practically and theoretically. The spirit of *The Society of the Spectacle* was *there*, though some had never fully understood it, or even read it. On the other hand, Debord and other Situationists were frequently the most sectarian, invariably falling out with allies – *especially* falling out with allies, being most ruthless with old friends and former comrades. 'Guy was a very tenacious person', Jean-Michel Mension, one of those ousted, remembered in his Situationist memoir *The Tribe*. 'He was already very hard – very strict in the way he conceived of existence with this person or that.' At the same time, there was a playful aspect to the manner in which he and his comrades lived. There 'were certainly jokers who became part of Guy's group merely because they were friends of so and so, people who had no business there and who lasted only six months or a year before Guy found them really idiotic and kicked them out.'

Debord also pointed the finger at his former pal Henri Lefebvre, denouncing him as an 'agent of recuperation'. Lefebvre pointed the finger back, likening Debord's 'cult of exclusion' to that of the Surrealist André Breton. 'I was never part of this group', Lefebvre said. 'I could have been, but I was careful, since I knew Guy's character and his manner, and the way he had of imitating André

May 1968 still
from the film
*The Society of the
Spectacle*, showing
Debord in
a white jacket
without glasses.

Breton, by expelling everyone in order to get at a pure and hard little core. In the end, the members of the Situationist International
were only Guy Debord, Raoul Vaniegem and Michèle Bernstein.'[12]
Debord, for his part, accused his former friend of stealing sı's ideas.
'A certain influence has been attributed to Lefebvre', he wrote in one
pamphlet, 'for the sı's radical theses that he surreptitiously copied,
but he reserved the truth of that critique for the past, even though
it was born out of the *present* more than out of his academic reflec-
tions on the past.'[13] Debord reckoned Lefebvre's take on the 1871
Paris Commune was almost entirely lifted from sı's 'Theses on
the Commune' (1962). 'This was a delicate subject', Lefebvre later
recalled in a 1987 interview.

> I was close to the Situationists . . . And then we had a quarrel
> that got worse and worse in conditions I don't understand too
> well myself . . . I had this idea about the Commune as a festival,
> and I threw it into debate, after consulting an unpublished
> document about the Commune that is at the Feltrinelli
> Institute in Milan. I worked for weeks at the Institute; I found
> unpublished documentation. I used it, and that's completely
> my right . . . Listen, I don't care at all about these accusations
> of plagiarism. And I never took the time to read what they

wrote about the Commune in their journal. I know that I was dragged through the mud.

The rift between Debord and Lefebvre is a complex topic, and its explanation involves some mixture of personality clash, political ideology and arguments over women. Plagiarism around the interpretation of the Commune is but one relatively minor strand. Deep down, Debord viewed Lefebvre as an old Leninist who continued to fraternize with the Party despite his expulsion. Meanwhile, Lefebvre got involved with several young women known to the Situationists, friends of Michèle Bernstein, one of whom, Nicole, became pregnant with Lefebvre's child. He was old enough to be her father several times over, and Debord et al. weren't impressed with what they saw as old Lefebvre's Don Juan pretensions.[14] For Lefebvre, Debord's dogmatism was too austere and ruthless. What's more, said Lefebvre, it was a dogmatism without a dogma, 'since the theory of situations, of the creation of situations, disappeared very quickly, leaving behind only the critique of the existing world, which is where it all started, with my *Critique of Everyday Life*'.[15] Perhaps in the end, despite their similar interpretations of urbanism and humanist Marxism, the two men were simply different personas: Debord was a man of the moon, cold and dark, pessimistic and destructive. It was at night when he had the power to create worlds. Lefebvre was a man of the sun, of creation, of light and optimism. In his 1959 autobiography, *La Somme et le reste*, Lefebvre describes himself 'surging from the depths, surfacing, a little flattened by heavy pressures. He breathes in the sunshine, opens himself, displays himself, comes alive again.'[16]

Both men, however, believed that the Commune of 1871 was some sort of historical antecedent of 1968. As Prussian forces at war with France surrounded Paris, for 73 days, between March and May, the city had become a liberated zone of people power. Amid carnivals and pranks, the barricades went up, even across

Haussmann's mighty boulevards. Freely elected workers, artists and small business owners were suddenly at the helm. Their rally cries were territorial and urban; their practice was festive and spontaneous. The Communards, until the National Guard crushed 20,000 of them, launched a revolt in culture and everyday life, demanded freedom and self-determination, and crushed Louis Napoleon's authority as he'd once crushed their freedom. They occupied the streets, shouted and sang for their 'right to the city'.

For the first time, it looked as if a working-class revolution wasn't merely possible, but imminent. The Situationists said that the 'Commune was the biggest festival of the nineteenth century' (thesis 2). 'Underlying the events of that spring of 1871 one can see the insurgents' feeling that they had become the masters of their own history, not so much on the level of "governmental" politics as on the level of their everyday life.'[1] 'The Commune', thesis 7 said, 'represents the only realization of a revolutionary urbanism to date.' It 'succumbed less to the force of arms', the next thesis explained, 'than to the force of habit'. 'Theoreticians who examine the history of this movement', continued thesis 11, importantly, 'can easily prove that the Commune was objectively doomed to failure and could not have been fulfilled. They forget that for those who really lived it, the fulfilment *was already there*' (emphasis in original). 'The audacity and inventiveness of the Commune', continued thesis 12, 'must obviously be measured not in relation to our time, but in terms of the prevailing political, intellectual and moral attitudes of its own time, in terms of the interdependence of all the prevailing banalities that it blasted to pieces.' 'The social war of which the Commune was one moment', concluded the penultimate thesis 13, 'is still being fought today. In the task of "making conscious the unconscious tendencies of the Commune" (Engels), the last word is still to be said.'

Ninety-seven years later, during the equally turbulent 'May-days' of 1968, history repeated itself on Paris's streets. In 1968 Debord and

Lefebvre duelled for an answer. The Nanterre sociologist claimed that the Situationists

> proposed not a concrete utopia, but an abstract one. Do they really imagine that one fine day or one decisive evening people will look at each other and say, 'Enough! We're fed up with work and boredom! Let's put an end to them!' and they will then proceed into eternal Festival and the creation of situations? Although this happened once, at the dawn of March 18, 1871, this combination of circumstances will not occur again.

'The '68 movement didn't come from the Situationists', Lefebvre insisted years later. 'The movement of March 22 was made up by students . . . It was an energetic group that took form as the events developed, with no programme, no project – an informal group, with whom the Situationists linked up, but it wasn't they who constituted the group.'[18]

In the wake of the '68 uprising, Debord released a film version of *The Society of the Spectacle*, dedicating it to his wife, Alice Becker-Ho, whose beautiful image, clad in flat cap, leaning on a wall with a cigarette drooping nonchalantly from her mouth, fills one frame. It evokes an Alice-cum-Brando's Johnny pose: Alice, whattya rebelling against? Whattya got? The film's dialogue closely follows Debord's original book text; but the rapid-fire captions, disarming classical music and exaggerated footage makes it visually stunning. As usual, there are battle scenes and moody vistas of Paris, spliced between images of Lenin, Stalin, Mao and Castro, all giving speeches; Debord plainly disapproves. There are news clips from the '68 Renault strike, with workers locked inside the factory by the unions; scenes from the Bourse alive with frenzied traders, participating in money mayhem; there's a vision of the Tower of Babel amid pitched battles from Vietnam and Watts, *circa* 1965; Paris's streets are ablaze, and students can be seen fighting cops; there are burning barricades at night, the storming of the Winter Palace in 1917, street altercations in Italy in the 1960s, Italian police leaping from jeeps, truncheoning a crowd of young people; West German security forces patrol another street, while Soviet tanks push back German workers in Berlin in June 1953.

There's also a shot of the Enragés-SI Committee, along with Debord himself, in that white jacket. Then a speech flashes up on the screen:

> Comrades, with the Sud-Aviation factory in Nantes being occupied for the last two days by workers and students of that town, and today extending in several factories, the Sorbonne Occupation Committee calls for the immediate occupation of all factories in France, and for the formation of workers' councils. Comrades, spread this word and reproduce it as fast as possible.

A subtitle appears in English, from Shakespeare's Henry v: 'We few, we happy few, we band of brothers.' Then, wall graffiti from an occupied Sorbonne: 'Run quickly comrade, the old world is behind you!'[19]

Afterwards, the film relays a speech from Alexis de Tocqueville's *Souvenirs*, from his eyewitness account of a similar uprising in Paris almost exactly 120 years earlier:

> From 25 February onwards, a thousand strange systems frantically take leave from the brains of innovators and spread in the troubled minds of the mob. It seems that, from the shock of the Revolution, society itself had been reduced to dust and one had entered into a competition for a new form that needed to raise an edifice in its place. Everyone proposed a plan of their own; this one produced in newspapers; that one on posters that would soon cover walls; another loudly proclaimed by word of mouth. One intended to destroy the inequality of wealth, another the

inequality of education – a third undertook to level the oldest of all inequalities, that between man and woman; one specifically rallied against poverty and indicated remedies for the torment of work that has tortured humanity since its earliest existence.[20]

Years later, Debord confessed he'd loved Tocqueville's *Souvenirs* on the revolution of 1848 because the latter 'had so well seen its weaknesses'.[21] He admired the conservative author of *Democracy in America* because the weaknesses he'd pinpointed, which eventually unhinged the 1848 workers' movement, applied so poignantly to its twentieth-century counterpart. *Souvenirs* revealed the bitterness of struggle during the February revolution and the subsequent 'June Days', when the *garde mobile* massacred the insurgents. Debord updated this tragedy, turning it not into farce but grist for his own diagnostic mill. Tocqueville was himself unseated in February from the Legislative Assembly, but resumed his post after re-election and after the 'party of order' recaptured power. Although he'd recognized the 'foolishness' of the 1848 revolutionary 'mob', he tried – at first anyway – to understand and sympathize with it, and even admired its participants. Before long, his hatred of socialism won out, and back in the Assembly he soon got tough, voting against amnesty for those convicted in the mobilizations; he also vetoed legislation limiting the working day to ten hours. For a while, Tocqueville served under Louis Napoleon's new presidency, until his *coup d'état* of 1851. The torn Tocqueville despised the right-wing authoritarianism of the Second Empire, and never forgave the man Marx called 'Crapulinski' for his affront to representative democracy and civil liberties.[22]

The film of *The Society of the Spectacle* sealed a magical era for Debord, begun in adolescence in Cannes in 1951 with the Lettrists, and concluding in middle age in 1972 in Paris, after the Situationists had come apart at the seams in their 'veritable split'.

But he regretted nothing. The dissolution of the Situationists, he said, marked their resounding success. 'Whoever considers the life of the SI', he contended, 'finds there the history of the revolution. Nothing has been able to sour it.'[23] It was how it had been for the Communards, who really lived it, whose fulfilment was already *there*. Fulfilment was already there for Debord, too: he really did live it in '68, and now it was over. Nothing could sour it. He'd never live permanently again in Paris. Where could he go? Where could he shelter as the 'repugnant Seventies' kicked in? He had told us in *In Girum Imus Nocte et Consumimur Igni* that he'd have to leave Paris. It had fallen to the enemy. He was a marked man now, an agitator, a villain, a fugitive; the French secret police began its dossier on him; they'd track him closely as he'd flee to Italy, to Spain, and of course to Champot. The media wouldn't be far behind. There was, it seemed, nobody for Debord to expel now, except himself.

As the dust from 1968 settled, emptiness prevailed in the ruins. Many *soixante-huitards* suddenly found themselves stuck between a rock and the hard place, between a degenerative past and an impossible future. For a moment, the dream of spontaneous freedom became real, in wide-awake time. An instant later, it disappeared in a puff of smoke, perhaps forever. In 1968 people demanded the impossible; soon 'the end of history' would grip. In 1967, the venerable year that *The Society of the Spectacle* revealed itself to the world, Jim Morrison of The Doors screamed: 'we want the world and we want it now!'; in 1977 punk Johnny Rotten of The Sex Pistols bawled a new *Zeitgeist*: 'no future, no future for you and me!' What had happened in those ten years? Debord himself never gave the question even a first thought. He was already wandering with Alice. But Rotten's cry was a final catharsis, a stark valedictory gesture to the heady 1960s – and a plague-on-your-house denunciation of the Coca-Cola realism to come. Those children of Marx, who'd been going round and round trying to overthrow spectacular society, eventually got consumed by it; they'd plunge down the same abyss they'd been staring down for far too long.

The street-fighting 1960s had shaped Debord, had left their imprint on his being. At the same time, he was ready to bid the decade farewell, happy to move on from those years of hope and days of rage. In an odd sense, too, Debord was a peculiar '68er since he was of an older stock, coming of age instead in the 1950s. Moreover, he often liked to brag that his disposition was even older than that, was more baroque, harking back to another century: his Marxism, we might say, went back to the future from the seventeenth-century. 'I was not converted by May 1968', he once confessed. 'I am an older bandit than that.'[24] Indeed, he liked to call himself 'Gondi', after the strange seventeenth-century Cardinal de Retz, Jean François Paul de Gondi.

Debord idolized Retz, the master of deception, the folk hero and trusted patron of Paris's poor and dangerous classes, who between 1648 and 1652 helped incite the street protests against Louis XIV, revolts that became known as 'The Fronde'. Retz welcomed the name *frondeur*, a term originally applied to rampaging gangs of street ruffians who brandished slings (*frondes*) and ran riot across medieval France. Seventeenth-century *frondeurs* took pride in wearing this once pejorative appellation; Retz and his coterie of aristocratic dissidents appropriated it in their risky revolt. Debord was a peculiarly distant cousin of Retz, as it were, many times removed; he was the cardinal's twentieth-century alter ego. Descriptions of Retz even bear an uncanny resemblance to Debord. The cardinal was small with a large head, had a squat body, short spindly legs and a bulbous nose. His eyesight was bad, very myopic. 'Madame de Carignan told the queen one day that I was very ugly', Retz wrote in his ten-volume *Mémoires*. 'It was perhaps the only time in her life that she didn't lie.'

The cardinal was an odd mix of Catholic holy man – who never actually believed – and libertine. He was a priest and a duellist, a courtier and a conspirator. He womanized while he spread the Gospel. 'He would save the soul of others while condemning his own to perdition.'[25] At the time, he was one of a handful of men who recognized the raw power of popular discontent, of the 'popular masses' rebelling against the punitive taxes levied by the rich on the poor. At any rate, he mobilized pulpit oratory, blending moral passion and political rhetoric, to arouse the people and to subvert the Church. Meanwhile, he tried to dislodge the monarchy, being loved by the people and distrusted by the crown. He simultaneously incited mob violence and earnestly preached peace. He was duplicitous and conniving, both worshipped and reviled, as he indulged in a life of intrigue and bewildering adventure.

At one point, 30,000 people followed him onto the barricades: 'Now everyone was following me', he recalled in those *Mémoires* that Debord loved so much, 'and it was just as well, for this swarming mass of refuse was armed to the teeth. I flattered them, I caressed them, I insulted them, I threatened them, and at last I convinced them.' After the civil war, Retz did several years of hard time at Vincennes prison. Later, almost broken, he was dispatched to the château of Nantes and placed under house arrest. But he deceived his captors and made off one tumultuous night, dislocating his shoulder en route, yet escaping to freedom. Eventually, he'd journey to Spain and then onwards to Italy, as Debord would three hundred years down the road. From then on, both men would lead, in exile, a fugitive and vagabond existence. Together, they'd become aesthetes of subversion and Debord the *frondeur* of our spectacular age.

4

Aesthete of Subversion

More is demanded to produce one wise man today, than seven
formerly; and more is needed to deal with a single individual in our
times, than with a whole people in the past.
Baltasar Gracián, *The Art of Worldly Wisdom*

The storms in the Haute-Loire move in rapidly, especially in
summer, in late afternoon. At first, the sun disappears behind dark
clouds that sneak up as the wind gusts. Soon trees begin to sway
back and forth, creaking in the breeze. Next, sudden flashes appear
on the horizon. The winds get stronger and stronger; everything
turns black. Lightning strikes, everything is lit up brilliantly white,
then claps of thunder. The rains come slowly, initially in large
drops, and you can smell the sweetness of raw earth rising. Then
mighty hailstones lash down. As the winds turn more violent, the
lone person, openly exposed to the monsoon, is defenceless.

These dramatic weather patterns aren't too dissimilar to storms
that break out across the economic and political landscape. Each,
after all, takes place when the temperature is hottest, when the
pressure dial approaches danger level. Often nobody pays attention
to the inclement forecast. In such heat, wealth accumulates,
business booms and stock prices grow, until, suddenly, the bubble
bursts and the heavens open. Crashes and storm clouds have
become increasingly frequent under capitalism since the early
1970s – since Debord embarked on his European wanderings. As

he fled post-'68 Paris, and as its new Platonic republic banned poets, storms began to hit global capitalism particularly hard. Debord observed a few of them indoors, from his Champot fortress under siege; he also weathered many more wandering in Italy and Spain.

The first dark cloud appeared in the summer of 1971, on a hot August day, when, without prior warning, President Richard Nixon devalued the dollar. He wrenched it from its gold standard mooring, heralding the United States's unilateral abandonment of the 1944 Bretton Woods agreement. Gone, practically overnight, was the system of financial and economic regulation that had been the mainstay of a quarter of a century of 'spectacular' capitalist expansion. It's impossible to imagine the long boom of the 1950s and '60s without this 1944 pact, without the free movement of capital being held in check, without stabilizing domestic management of trade and finance. Yet, 25 years on, as the US economy bore the brunt of a costly war in Vietnam, a chill wind started to waft back westwards.

Indeed, the year 1971 ushered in an American balance-of-trade deficit: the nation was importing more than it exported. Nixon knew fixed exchange rates couldn't be sustained, not without overvaluing the dollar, not without losing competitive ground. So he let the dollar drift, devalued it, and loosened Bretton Woods's grip. World currency hereafter oscillated; capital could now more easily slush back and forth across national frontiers. A deregulated, unstable capitalism had had its birth pangs, a terrible beauty was about to be born. And if that wasn't enough, the 1973 oil embargo by the petroleum exporting countries (OPEC) – a punitive measure in the face of the Arab-Israeli conflict – rained another bout of thunder and lightening. From $1.90, the price of a barrel of oil skyrocketed to $9.76. (In 1979, because of Iran–Iraq squabbles, it upped again, from $12.70 to $28.76 per barrel.)

The halcyon days of cheap fuel were effectively over. Violent breezes battered every advanced economy. Storms turned into deep, soggy recessions; oil price hikes couldn't be absorbed by assorted economies already on the brink. In 1975, unable to fund its public services, unable to cope with increased energy costs, New York City declared itself bankrupt. The fiscal crisis of the state pervaded every level of government, as did public sector strikes, whose workers weren't going to get wet without a fight. In 1978–9 Britain underwent a 'winter of discontent'. Refuse and utility workers lobbied James Callaghan's Labour government for cost-of-living pay rises. Power cuts, rubbish mountains and rank-and-file acrimony greeted the Prime Minister's austerity appeals: Labour's Keynesianism, its capitalism with a human face, was about to perish forever.

Elsewhere, economic storms betokened other political unrest. In Italy, where Debord sojourned at the beginning of the 1970s, extra-parliamentary volatility became the new disorder filling the party political void, flourishing in the ruins of state-managed capitalism. In 1969 Italy saw a 'hot autumn' of labour unrest, its most sizzling class struggle in the post-war era. Wildcat strikes and wide-scale stoppage paralysed the country. Workers demanded better pay and more respect, or else. Sabotage occurred at the Fiat factory in Turin; then at the Pirelli plant in Milan; then at a hundred others elsewhere. And then, in December 1969, to cap it all, a bomb exploded at a bank in the Piazza Fontana, near Milan's busy cathedral, killing sixteen people, decapitating a few and maiming many more. Police immediately arrested two left-leaning anarchists; but, by 1971, they'd discover that, actually, neo-fascists had been the culprits, probably with the government's blessing, and probably aided by Italy's secret police, the dreaded SID. With the centre-left coalition government in tatters, unable to handle strikes, sabotage, scandals and bombings, to say nothing of post-1973 recession and inflation, 'extremist' factions, both left and right, came to the fore.

The Red Brigade became the most notorious left-wing species, kindred souls of Germany's Baader-Meinhof Gang, and they denounced everything and everyone: the government, the senile Italian Communist Party (PCI) – who, Red Brigaders said, had long reneged on the revolutionary struggle and had fossilized Italian Marxist politics. In the Red Brigade's hands, class struggle took on a violent 'Leninist' turn, and necessarily meant vanguard militancy and armed guerilla warfare. By 1970 they'd gone underground. Soon they would infiltrate the 'red' factories of Milan, conduct sabotage, burn automobiles, plant bombs and mastermind political kidnappings. Their campaign rapidly became a campaign of self-annihilation, something parasitic, internally divisive and debilitating for radical Left solidarity. Soon the Red Brigade became Public Enemy Number One, fervently dismissed by the authorities as crazy terrorists.

They were dismissed in other circles, too, especially by 'Censor', aka Gianfranco Sanguinetti, the mysterious author of the pamphlet 'The Real Report on the Last Chance to Save Capitalism in Italy' (1975). Sanguinetti adopted the sly alias 'Censor' to assume the role of a cool-headed, ruthless Italian capitalist, framing the 'Italian question' from their reactionary standpoint. (The pseudonym was borrowed from Marcus Porcius Cato, a Roman historian and statesman, who'd fought against Hannibal and philosophized about austerity and bygone Puritanism.) Five hundred copies of the pamphlet were mailed to Italy's elite businessmen, economists, politicians and journalists, urging them to co-opt the reformist Communist Party and career unionists, while getting tough on the 'autonomous' revolutionary workers' movement – before it was too late. The Red Brigade, Censor said, was marginal and insignificant; the real dangers came from the loose-knit and anarchistic autonomous groups, who touted the illegality of wage-labour and who saw the Italian crisis not as an economic crisis but as a *crisis of the economy*.

All along, though, Censor was really a crypto-Situationist and advocate of exactly the thing he preached against: workers' self-management. His ostensible right-wing frontal attack, which

summoned up Machiavelli and Clausewitz for guidance, was
a cunning rearguard left-wing war of position. It was a manifesto
utilizing the kind of logic Machiavelli and Clausewitz both
invoked: know thy enemy! And Sanguinetti's mentor and comrade-
in-arms was none other than Guy Debord himself, who, in a letter
dated 4 April 1978, had said:

> I knew a man who used to spend his time amongst the *sfacciate
> donne fiorentine,* and who loved to carouse with the low company
> of all the drunkards of the bad quarters. He understood all that
> went on. He showed it once. One knows that he can still do it.
> He is therefore considered by some as the most dangerous man
> in Italy.

The bomb at the Piazza Fontana, Sanguinetti's Censor insisted,
'had, in its way, a salutary affect by completely disorienting the
workers and the country as a whole.' After the bombings, amid the
disarray, 'one never saw such reciprocal support from all institutional forces – such solidarity between political parties and the government, between the government and the forces of order, between
the forces of order and the union.'[1] The Italian state, he added,
continually defends itself 'from phantom enemies – red or black
according to the mood of the moment'. But it never wants to 'confront the problems posed by the *real enemy* of the society founded
on property and work. Our state wastes its time combating the
phantoms that it created, waiting to create an alibi that would
maintain its innocence for its real desertion.'[2] 'To banish a present
danger,' Sanguinetti's Censor said, provoking both his Left and
Right audience, and citing Machiavelli, 'irresolute princes most
often follow the neutral path, and most often they lose themselves.'[3]

Censor's text appeared three years before the most phantasmal
act of terrorism struck: the Red Brigade's abduction, and subsequent execution, of a well-known Italian politician and ex-Prime

Minister, Aldo Moro. Though no longer a government minister, the Christian Democratic Moro was seen as somebody who could build bridges and affect an 'historic compromise'. In the 1960s he'd been an anti-communist centre-left; in the 1970s he vacillated around pragmatic consensus. Now out of office, though still prominent on TV as a political commentator, he strove to hand an olive branch to the communists.

On the morning of 16 March 1978, vindicated and celebrating the advent of a new coalition government led by the Christian Democrat Giulio Andreotti, with the blessing of the Italian Communist Party (PCI), Moro was scheduled to appear in Parliament. His dark blue Fiat 130 had made the three-mile trek through Rome's streets, from Moro's home, a thousand times before. Only this time, it was skilfully intercepted, ostensibly by an innocent reversing car. But it was a professional hit. Moro's chauffeur and two bodyguards were killed instantly by submachine-gun fire. Another got a bullet in the back of the head as he desperately crawled out of the car; a fourth bled to death hours later in hospital. Moro himself was whisked off, unhurt, by a speeding Fiat. For the next few months, his whereabouts and fate dominated Italian media and politics.[4]

The day after the abduction, the Red Brigade phoned, admitting responsibility. After a while it mailed other communiqués: Moro, they said, was held in 'the people's prison', awaiting trial as a 'henchman of the multinationals'. He was, they claimed, 'closely tied to imperialist circles'; for 'thirty years' he had 'oppressed the Italian people'.[5] Red Brigade letters came in thick and fast: a second, a third, a fourth and fifth, then a sixth, seventh and eighth. And then, with the ninth, came the dramatic, and dreaded, verdict: 'Aldo Moro is guilty and is therefore condemned to death.' On 9 May 1978 two Red Brigaders, equipped with a Scorpion submachine-gun and a Beretta pistol, riddled the Christian Democratic politician's body with bullets. Moro was later dumped in the back of a red Renault, and parked in a spot almost exactly halfway between the headquarters of his own party and the PCI's.

Debord followed these events and their repercussions closely. He drafted a new Preface to the fourth Italian edition of *The Society of the Spectacle*, barely six months after Moro's deadly 'historic compromise'. He expressed considerable interest in the Italian situation: first, with respect to the Italian reception of his book; second, to the antics of the Red Brigade, whom he deemed 'the Stalinist trade union police'. Meanwhile, he got to know Italy well and was always fascinated by its dramas and shenanigans. He slowly learnt the language, became absorbed by its wine, literature and culture, and even bragged about his roots – his half-sister, remember, had an Italian father. 'Italy', he'd said,

> is the most modern laboratory for international counter-revolution. Other governments descended from the old pre-spectacular bourgeois democracy, look with admiration at the Italian government, for the impassiveness it knows how to maintain at the centre of all tumultuous degradations, and for the tranquil dignity with which it wallows in the mud.[6]

But, in the factories of this very same country, his book also found its best readers. 'For their absenteeism, for their wildcat strikes that aren't appeased by no particular concession, for their lucid refusal to work, and for their contempt for the law and for all statist parties', Italian workers, he noted, 'are an example to their comrades of all other countries'. They 'know the subject well enough by practice to have been able to benefit from the theses of *La Société du Spectacle*, even when they read only mediocre translations of them.'[7] Still, Debord reviled the Red Brigade itself, yet understood them ironically: he knew that if the Situationist International had lived beyond 1972, it too would have been branded a 'terrorist' group and tarred with the same brush.

He also thought the Moro affair 'a mythological opera with great machinations'. 'Terrorist heroes', he said, turned 'into foxes to ensnare their prey, into lions to fear nobody for as long as they can, and into sheep so as not to derive from this *coup d'état* anything harmful to the regime they feign to defy.'[8] The Red Brigade, Debord added, were blessed by good luck: they dealt with the world's most incompetent police force, some of whom had actually infiltrated the Red Brigade, without apparent hindrance. The Red Brigade's 'illogical and blind terrorism', served only to embarrass itself; gladly, the mass media seized upon it and the Italian state used it – indeed, nourished it – to bolster its repressive power. In this sense, Red Brigade politics was a 'spectacular politics of terrorism', playing straight into the hands of the right-wing media and Stalinists, whom, Debord said, the Red Brigade always refused to denounce. Ultimately, the Red Brigade's sole function was to disconcert and discredit those workers who really did want to smash the state. And, from his underground Italian lair, smashing the state was still top of Debord's agenda.

Debord gives us a few hints of what he got up to in Italy, where he wasn't well received by everyone. Assuredly, he drank a lot of Italian wine and grappa, while trying hard not to avoid dangerous encounters. Now, however, his Situationist rebel-rousing days were done; he subverted freelance instead, without affiliation. He tells us he lived principally in Florence, in the old artisan Oltrarno district, in an apartment in a fourteenth-century building along the Via delle Caldaie. In Florence, too, he 'had the good fortune to know the *sfacciate donne fiorentine*'. 'There was this little Florentine', he said in *Panégyrique*,

> who was so graceful. At night, she would cross the river to come to San Frediano. I fell in love very unexpectedly, perhaps because of her beautiful, bitter smile. And I told her, in brief: 'Do not stay silent, for I come before you as a stranger and a

traveler. Grant me some refreshment before I go away and am here no more.'[9]

At the time, Italy 'was once again losing its way: it was necessary to regain sufficient distance from its prisons, where those who stayed too long at the revels of Florence ended up'.[10] So our stranger and traveller hid himself away for a while in the verdant hills of Chianti, in another old house, behind another high stone wall. He and Alice had a penchant for things ancient, for places grand yet shabby, aristocratic yet proletarian. It was an odd mix; somehow they managed to pull it off and to assume all the regal airs of the dangerous classes. Was Guy a pilgrim descending into hell, or someone ascending up the mountain of purgatory, reaching upwards toward paradise? The Dantesque inflection seems apt. He'd read the Florentine *maestro*, who'd similarly been banished from his native city. 'What force or fatality', Debord asked in *Panégyrique*, citing Dante's *Purgatory* (Canto v), 'took you so far from Campaldino/ that one had never known your burial place.' 'He goes in search of freedom', Dante had written elsewhere (Canto i), 'and how dear that is,/ the man who gives up life for it well knows.'

The other Florentine to beseech Debord was, of course, Machiavelli, the crafty Renaissance theorist. It was a common defect of men in fair weather, Machiavelli warned, to take no thought of storms.[11] Debord thought a lot about storms, especially those that broke out in fair weather. Machiavelli helped him ride a few, and revealed the lessons of shrewdness, not simply force, in political manoeuvring. Debord's Machiavelli didn't so much preach about power as lecture about survival through waiting and strategizing, trickery and daring. Machiavelli taught Debord about deception and discretion. Indeed, he appropriated Machiavelli's sixteenth-century *Discourses* and *The Prince* as handbooks toward liberty not autocracy. Machiavelli suggested a prince had 'to know well how to employ the nature of the beasts'. Princes should be able to assume the nature of the fox and the lion; for while the latter cannot escape the traps laid for him, the former cannot defend himself against wolves. A prince should be a fox, to know the traps and snares; and a lion, to be able to frighten the wolves; for those who simply hold to the nature of the lion do not understand their business.[12]

In 1971, just as Richard Nixon devalued the dollar, Debord discovered a real-life prince among men: the left-leaning media mogul, impresario and movie producer Gérard Lebovici. Soon, a budding friendship took hold. The French daily *France-Soir* once described Lebovici as 'a genius in business, the most important agent-producer in French cinema'. Lebovici – or 'le roi Lebo' (King Lebo), as he was called, at once fondly and pejoratively – headed the Artmedia casting agency, whose list included towering figures of French film: Jean-Paul Belmondo, Jeanne Moreau, Gérard Depardieu and Catherine Deneuve. He was suave and sophisticated, and rich and cultured as only Parisians can be. He was a handsome playboy with Left sensibilities, who lived a glamorous life yet avoided the limelight. He also controlled a small publishing house, Champ Libre (Free Field), launched after May 1968, which dealt with off-beat radical texts, often obscure books that gave the finger to the same establishment that had made Lebovici wealthy.

He and Debord were almost identical ages, both brilliantly intelligent, *bon vivants* with under-class tendencies. Lebovici was passionately interested in the Situationists, and he and the ex-Situ *chef* genuinely hit it off. Champ Libre wasted no time in republishing *The Society of the Spectacle*; Lebovici bankrolled Debord's film version a year later, and picked up the tab for *In Girum Imus Nocte et Consumimur Igni* a few years after that. In fact, Lebovici financed the costs of airing all Debord's other movies, even buying a little cinema, Studio Cujas, in the Latin Quarter dedicated to Guy's cinematic works. Plainly, our aesthete of subversion had found both a prince and a fairy godmother.

Before long, the word got out about their friendship. In intellectual circles, they became the talk of the town. Then the tabloids and the glossies weighed in, ever eager for mindless gossip. Inevitably, fact blurred into fiction. Wasn't Lebovici a man now under the influence, besotted with Debord, who was steering the millionaire producer towards extremist organizations, like the Red Brigade, like the Baader-Meinhof? Didn't Lebovici finance them because of his taste for scandal and provocation? Wasn't he the 'great prostitute of spectacular terrorism', funding ultra-leftist cliques, as one right-wing newspaper put it, under the watchful eye of police and Mafia alike? Wasn't Debord the *éminence grise* who really controlled Champ Libre's editorial department? In 1974, its four publishing staff, fronted by Gérard Guégan, were all ousted; Debord was accused of masterminding the *coup d'état* at Champ Libre. Yet, 'why was it necessary', he asked, 'to believe in my influence to explain an event so trifling, which I was totally estranged from, and that I only learned about months later in Italy, where I was then living?'[13]

Years afterwards, Guégan still apparently bore a grudge. After Debord's death, he penned a thin, rather scurrilous text, whipped off almost overnight, entitled *Guy Debord est mort, le Che aussi. Et alors?* ('Debord is dead and Che too. So what?').[14] In it, Guégan recalls getting an afternoon phone call advising: 'Debord is dead.' Guégan shrugs his shoulders indifferently, and remembers receiving a similar call, from the same person, a few months earlier about the death of another hard-core drinker, Charles Bukowski. First-time tragedy, he muses, second-time farce. Guégan, though, must have had a late night himself, because he was a full month out on the actual date of Debord's suicide. Debord, for his own part, once claimed not to have known or met Guégan. Still, he'd read Guégan's *Les Irréguliers*. 'It's a sorry thing', commiserated Debord, 'like everything Guégan writes.'[15]

Lebo, like his pal Guy, was a man both ahead of and behind the times; he was an entrepreneur as well as a knight, who seemed to epitomize all the grace and elegance of Tuscan virtue outlined in Castiglione's *The Book of the Courtier*. Together, Lebovici and Debord became prince and courtier; often it was difficult to tell who was who, and who influenced the other. Both, as Castiglione wrote in 1528, were necessarily cautious and wise. 'Thus, gentleness is most striking in a man who is valiant and impetuous; and his boldness seems greater when accompanied with modesty, so his modesty is enhanced and made more evident by his boldness.' Hence, 'to talk little', said Castiglione, 'and to do much, and not to praise oneself with deeds that are praiseworthy, but tactfully to dissimulate them, serves to enhance both the one virtue and the other in anyone who knows how to employ this method discreetly.'[16]

Whether as prince or courtier, Debord now had a trusty patron for his enterprises and wanderings. From Florence to the hills of Tuscany, onwards into Spain, Guy and Alice took flight, journeying to Barcelona, to Madrid, to Cadiz, and to Seville. Debord adored Spain as he adored Italy. From Italian political intrigue, he now enveloped himself in warm Spanish air. He went in search of sunshine and *duende*, for a dash of the demonic, for Gypsies and flamenco, for music and dance, for sensuality and folklore, for what the Spanish poet Federico García Lorca dubbed 'deep song'. Paris had had its deep song taken away; Debord wanted it back, in spite of the spectacle. In Barcelona, he followed Orwell and Genet into shady bars near the Ramblas, where he'd sometimes rendezvous with Lebovici, in the freer post-Franco period, after 1975. In these *caves*, the lost found themselves and the found lost themselves. Soon, too, Debord would discover *duende* in Andalusia, in Seville, in its darkest bramble patches, amongst its wildest songs and most decadent life.

No map will help anyone find *duende*, Lorca warned. It burns in the blood, like a poultice of broken glass; it exhausts, rejects geometry, leans on human pain and smashes styles. Great artists of the south of Spain, especially of Andalusia, whether they sing or dance or bullfight, know nothing comes unless the *duende* comes. The commodified world of modern capitalism, Debord knew, killed *duende*, neutered it, doused it, took away its feeling. A life of wealth and abundance perversely materializes into nothingness, into an air-conditioned nightmare, anodyne and unadventurous, a world devoid of real sensuality. 'The duende's arrival', Lorca wrote, 'always means a radical change in forms. It brings to old planes unknown feelings of freshness, with the quality of something newly created, like a miracle.' Spain is moved by *duende*, he said, 'for it is a country of ancient music and dance where the *duende* squeezes the lemons of death – a country of death, open to death. Everywhere else, death is an end. Death comes, and they draw the curtains. Not in Spain. In Spain they open them.'[17]

Death is the subject of Spain's best-known and most popular poem, *Verses on the Death of his Father*, written in the 1470s by Jorge Manrique. Manrique, like most Spanish writers of that century, belonged to one of the elite Castilian families. His father, Don Rodrigo, whose death is lamented in the stanzas, was a famous military officer; Jorge's uncle, Gomez Manrique, was a poet of distinction. Jorge himself, who died at the tender age of 39 defending Queen Isabella's crown, was really a minor scribe, penning mostly trite lines. But, somehow, through his elegy on his dead father, he 'was able to write a poem that sums up the accumulated feelings of an entire age'. These words are those of the English writer Gerald Brenan, another lover of Spain and one-time Andalusian resident, from *The Literature of the Spanish People* (1951). It appeared in French under Champ Libre's imprint, doubtless at Debord's behest, alongside Brenan's other great book, his Spanish Civil War history *The Spanish Labyrinth* (1943).

Debord cites Brenan's summation of Manrique from *The Literature of the Spanish People* in his preface to *Stances sur la mort de son père*. Perhaps, as age 50 neared and drink began to take its toll, the

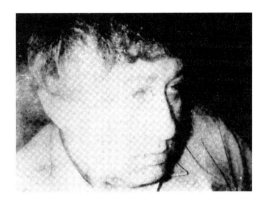

Debord aged 45; a still from his film *In Girum Imus Nocte Et Consumimur Igni*.

ex-Situationist had become aware of his own mortality. For during the late 1970s he'd quietly and painstakingly translated into French Manrique's Castilian *Coplas*. It was an amazing linguistic achievement, particularly for somebody 'who had never judged highly the frequenting of universities' and 'who isn't in any degree a Hispanist'. Nevertheless, the circumstances of 'his itinerant life', he added, 'and of his less socially accepted occupations', made him more than qualified to capture the true flavour and meaning of this Spanish classic.[18] 'When one has had the pleasure of knowing the true Spain', Debord wrote, 'from one or two admirable figures whom she has produced in the history of this century, and in those preceding, one also had to love its language, and its poetry.'[19]

In 1980, when Champ Libre released Debord's *Stances*, it disclosed his deeply ontological connection with Spain, as well as a 48-year-old rebel's connection with himself. Perhaps he'd recognized that his only remaining strategy was to dig in grimly, to await the end with loyal obstinacy, because to struggle against death was futile. 'The earthly life', Debord said, 'is still seen as a voyage towards another eternal life; but one senses [in Manrique], above all, its brevity, the triumph of death, the dissolution and loss of all that exists one moment in the world.'[20] This post-Machiavellian *froideur* conjures up magnificently the spirit of Manrique – a spirit Debord wanted to haunt our age as

much as it haunted him. I have tried to be faithful to Debord's French
translation of Castilian Spanish in my English translation:

> Arouse yourself, sleeping soul
> and step out of your torpor,
>
> Contemplating
> How life has passed,
> And how death arises,
> By surprise;
> How pleasure slips away . . .

And in verse III we hear the futility of wealth:

> There are rivers, our lives,
> That descend toward the sea
> Of death.
> There go the lordships themselves

And in verse XVI we hear a romantic lament:

> Where is he, the king Don Juan?
> And the princes of Aragon,
> Where are they?
> Where are so many of the amorous?
>
> Where did their ruses lead?
> What did they find?
> Were they only vain shadows,
> That passed through the grass
>
> Like seasons,
> The duels and tournaments,
> The ornaments and embroideries,
> And crests?

And in verse xxvi Don Rodrigo and his type are immortalized:

> What friend for his friends!
> For his people and parents, what a
> Lord! What an
> Enemy for the enemy!
>
> What leader of the fearless,
> And the steadfast!
> What judgement for the wise!
> For the pleasant, what grace!
>
> What grand sense!
> Mild to his dependents
> But, for the mean and harmful,
> What a lion!

And in verse xxxiv, we hear the virtue of strength and reputation:

> Saying to him: 'Honest Knight,
> Flee this deceptive world
> Of reflections;
> And that your heart so firm
>
> Display its celebrated strength
> This instant.
> Since for you health, life,
> Do not compare with
>
> Reputation,
> That virtue so taut
> For withstanding this affront
> Which summons you.'

The morbidity of the verse is offset by grandeur of the will. 'One needs to recognize some more modern traits', Debord pointed out. 'One needs to fight for the "true king"', he said, 'who is the one you've created yourself.'[21] Maybe, here, there's some punctuation between the young and mature radical, an epistemological break in himself and in his thought? For, as in 1980, it seems that Debord wants to wrench himself out of the political realm altogether, and propel his body and mind elsewhere, into medieval metaphysics. In one sense, *Stances* marks a political withdrawal, an abandoning of the collective project Debord affirmed so ardently in his Situationist years. In another, it exhibits him ratcheting up the political stakes. It shows him getting stronger, not weaker, as the spectacle gets stronger. He tells us he's more devoted than ever before to the 'true king', to oneself, against all odds. He reminds us that virtue and reputation will win out in the end, despite everything. If the spectacle is going to erode all higher values, convert everyone and everything into exchange values, he's going to invent new values, older values, longer-ranged values, about virtue and stoicism in the face of death and imminent old age. Meanwhile, he's going to wander with Alice, amongst peripatetic heroes and Romany adventurers, knowing that there are certain things he can't avoid, and knowing this means he can wander more freely.

Guy and Alice greatly admired Romany culture and each was absorbed in its tradition. Throughout the 1970s they seemed happiest themselves on the high road, in flight. They'd read George Borrow, the quirky nineteenth-century 'Romany Rye', an English gent who'd befriended Gypsies, and who'd lived amongst them and knew their tongue. Borrow's autobiographical tales of open roads, empty fields, dense undergrowth and Romany lore spoke volumes to kindred free spirits.[22] He taught himself half-a-dozen languages and, between 1835 and 1840 journeyed to Spain under the employ of the Bible Society; in *The Bible in Spain*, a book that made his name, his love of the *zincali* and of Spain shone more than his salesmanship or proselytizing. Borrow was a veritable 'man in black', a renegade after Guy's and Alice's own hearts. He was a *lavengro*, a gifted 'word-smith', an autodidact philologist who similarly recognized the joy and power of language, of argot and patois, of a natural, authentic literary beauty.

Borrow, like Guy and Alice, was fascinated by the colloquial speech of 'the dangerous classes'. He likewise knew how to put idiom into practice, learning his craft in wandering, not just in books. He was the first to challenge stereotypes about the Roma; and in books like *Lavengro* (1851) and *Romany Rye* (1857), and with real-life characters like Jasper Petulengro (a *maestro* horseman and sage) and Isopel Berners (a striking, eighteen-year-old six-foot Gypsy belle), he popularized their truer nature. They are 'widely different in their appearance from other people', Borrow wrote in *Lavengro*. 'Not so much in dress, for they are clad something after the fashion of rustic jockeys, but in their look . . . no ruddy cheeks, no blue quiet glances belong to them; their features are dark, their locks long, black and shining, and their eyes are wild . . . heroically beautiful, but wild, wild, wild.'[23]

The Gypsies whom Borrow described in *Lavengro* first arrived on British shores around 1500, in a trek begun five centuries earlier in India. Their westwards shift, across the Middle East, into the Byzantine Empire, and onwards to the Balkans and to continental Europe, was a restless tale of liberty and woe, of flight and exile, of wretchedness and spirit. They reputedly reached Constantinople in 1068; by 1320 they were well established in the Peloponnese. At the beginning of the fifteenth century they'd made it to Venice and Rome. In 1417 they'd hit Germany; in 1419, France; in 1425 they'd arrive in Spain. And yet, everywhere they went Gypsies were treated as pariah peoples. Their nomadic lifestyles threatened governments, whose rule had a prerequisite of order and stability; their features, their clothes, their habits and trades – horse-trading, blacksmiths, fortune-telling, circus performing, juggling, etc. – were disdained by normal 'settled' types.

The Debords affirmed the sensual and irrepressible *joie de vivre* of Gypsy lore that has endured despite centuries of persecution. One of their friends, Tony Gatlif, a Paris-based, Algerian-born film-maker, himself of Gypsy descent, has helped this cultural tradition flourish. It was Gatlif who turned Guy and Alice on to the magical world of the Roma, with memorably luscious portraits of Gypsies like *Latcho Drom* (1993), a documentary of dance and music, which featured alongside the premier public (and posthumous) screening on Canal + of *Guy Debord, son art et son temps* in January 1995.

Latcho Drom, or 'Safe Trip', maps the meandering 1,000-year Gypsy migration, from the golden sands of Rajasthan, haunting Kasbahs on the Nile, misty quays of Istanbul, bleak wintry cityscapes of Romania and Hungary, to the crowded peasant cafés in France and sun-drenched hills of Andalusia. Nowhere does Gatlif utilize actors in this musical odyssey; detail is authentic and real – the toothless grins, the pathos and squalor, the ecstatic chants and creaking violins, the vulgarity and the innocence, the melodies and the melodramas. 'You', a subtitle near the end of *Latcho Drom* says, 'are a stork who has settled on the earth; me, I am a bird who has been cast there.' In Gatlif's films, even trees have *duende*.

Alice herself, under her maiden name Becker-Ho, has become an authority on Gypsy culture and Romany – the language, she says, 'of those who know'. She's published several critically acclaimed books, *Les Princes du Jargon* (1990), *L'Essence du Jargon* (1994) and *Du Jargon héritier en Bastardie* (2002), and presented another, *Paroles de Gitans* (2000), on their hybrid tongue and disappearing world. Romany itself is a genuine language, not just a dialect or an argot. Its origins can actually be traced to Sanskrit; but as these wandering peoples spread westwards, they appropriated many 'loanwords' en route, blending and mixing and hybridizing Hebrew, Greek, German and

Romance languages, forging them into their own distinctive voice. In *Les Princes du Jargon*, Alice claimed that the 'slang' of every European vagabond group and the criminal 'dangerous classes', from the Middle Ages onwards, has an ascertainable base in Romany. This 'secretive and deliberately disguised language', she said, 'had been created initially with the help of that spoken by Gypsies, instead of deriving, as had long been maintained, from various national patois.' Hence Gypsy language 'emerges here as a mother tongue, as important to etymological studies as Latin or Greek'.[24]

Slang, said Alice, is popular speech, the everyday language of real men and women; often, too, its camouflage, a lexicon of dissimulation and secrecy, beyond the reach of jargon, which is created by intellectuals and specialists, by people with power and wealth. Jargon is 'like the colours of a team, while slang makes up the colour of a high wall, sheltered by popular phrases – like the knowing crowd, closing around itself, to protect a fugitive'.[25] It is the vocabulary of the urban dispossessed, and that's why she and husband Guy dig slang so much. It provokes and riles, is profane and rough and defies authority. It doesn't lay out a single screen, 'but is a play of mirrors and lighting'. It 'amuses or menaces'; it is, Alice reckoned, 'the power of words that recalls always that it is dangerous to speak: sometimes too much, sometimes not enough'.[26] The notion of 'the outsider' is crucial in the formation of slang, and here Gypsies come into their own, bringing into the linguistic fray 'their experiences of free men and nomads'. To that degree, Romany makes up one of the largest currents of slang, a major confluence in what Alice called a 'delta' configuration, whose tributaries include Hebrew-German, Greek, Armenian, Turkish, Arabic and Slavic.

Romany culture has deep roots in Arles, the Roman-Gaul capital of Provence, where Alice and Guy lived at the beginning of the 1980s. They lodged in a spacious first-floor apartment at 33 rue de l'Hôtel de Ville, in the old centre. Nestling on the east bank of the Rhône and gateway to the untamed Camargue, Arles' mild climate and radiant

Provençal light had inspired Van Gogh to shack up there a hundred years earlier. Arles Gypsies, who hark back to the 1430s, doubtless favoured Provence for its weather; they also liked the relative hospitality that the then-independent country offered as France battled against England in the Hundred Years War. In modern Arles, suntanned Gypsies continue to share space with rowdy Camargue cowboys and fearless matadors who regularly battle bulls in the town's 12,000-seat, first-century Roman amphitheatre. And that most famous Gypsy band ever, Gipsy Kings, equally hail from Arles. (By the time their smash hit 'Bamboleo' reverberated around every European bar and nightclub, Guy would be in no shape to dance.)

Although his mind was dark, Debord had a desire for sunshine in everyday life. Alice's antique-dealing brother, Eugène Becker-Ho, had a big fifteenth-century manor house in Saint-Pierre-du-Mont, but Debord said he wasn't attracted by the weather in Normandy. He preferred warmth. For much of the 1980s he and Alice would winter in Arles and summer in their Champot farmhouse. It was a nice split routine; everything, Debord insisted, is less costly for those who have taste. Arles today has narrow, higgledy-piggledy congested streets, one-way systems and hoards of tourists stomping around everywhere. A lot of old properties have terracotta rooftops; some houses are painted in bright primary colours; others are dull and shabby; all are cracked and crumbling. Tacky tourist stores jostle with trendy boutiques and graffiti-laden walls, making the glamour feel strangely seedy, an unappealing mix of kitsch wealth and squalour. Twenty-five-years ago, when Guy and Alice were here, things may have been different.

Walking down a narrow alley off the place du Forum, near the Café de Nuit, a horrible re-creation of the café Van Gogh immortalized, you reach the rue de l'Hotel de Ville; if you make a sharp right turn number 33 suddenly appears: a faded, once-grand, two-storey eighteenth-century building with a big oak front door, which has seen better days. The plasterwork around the doorframe is falling apart and nameless doorbells give no inkling of who lives there. On one side, a spattering of graffiti on a dishevelled wall; on the other, a *bourgeoise* fashion store. An apt Debordian metaphor perhaps, as he straddled the low and high life – a schism best incarnated by his friend Gérard Lebovici. A few yards along the same block is the magnificent twelfth-century Romanesque cathedral of St Trophime, with its carved stone portal depicting the Last Judgment. A series of trumpeting angels welcome worshippers and tourists through a giant red door. Facing the cathedral, the centrepiece of the place de la République, is the palatial seventeenth-century Town Hall, designed after Versailles. It's a bizarrely central and public location for Debord to inhabit, especially for somebody so secret, so guarded.

He and Alice had neither a TV nor a telephone there. Apparently, they sometimes watched television with a next-door neighbour. The unsuspecting Madame took the debonair Guy for a local bank employee! If Debord rarely went out, it was probably because of the paparazzi, who'd camp outside the building, awaiting a precious glimpse of the infamous man of the shadow. It became a game of hide and seek. 'I would certainly be a bad strategist of the urban milieu', he joked,

> if I did not know how to outmanoeuvre photographers. Always well accompanied, I was able to go out, eat at a restaurant, wander the city, without a single one of these bunglers – who are used to forcing stars out of their hiding – knowing how to meet up with me or daring to venture close enough to take a picture and get a worthwhile image. I do not think, having watched their antics, that I was sent the cream of the profession.[27]

It was behind these fraying Arles shutters that Debord planned another film, a mammoth, epic, cinematic undertaking on his great labour of love: Spain. 'Evading all clichés', he professed, the film would 'translate to screen not everything foreigners (Europeans,

Americans, Japanese, etc.) could imagine on the question, and not more than the Spanish themselves could believe, but: *what Spain really is*.'[28] It would begin in the fifteenth century and move towards the present day. He envisaged a portrait lasting between two and four hours, something that 'would eventually be destined to play in local movie houses and be broadcast on TV stations (cables, satellites, etc.). It might eventually entail some reconstituted parts in costumes, but must take into account contemporary Spain.' Above all, 'for diverse historical and evident cultural reasons', the film, he said, must centre on Andalusia.[29]

In October 1982 he signed a contract with Soprofilms, Lebovici's offshoot company, who agreed to finance the film in its entirety. With all the paperwork in place, with everything 'read and approved', Debord could return to Spain to research detail. He now seemed scheduled to make a dramatic screen comeback, re-entering the cinematic limelight in what appeared a curious machination with the mainstream. But the world, lamentably, would never see its like. On the morning of 7 March 1984, the project received a mortal setback. The whole of France awoke to some startling and shocking news: the agent and cinema producer Gérard Lebovici, aged 51, was found dead in an underground parking lot beneath avenue Foch in Paris's 16th *arrondissement*. He was slumped over the front seat of his Renault 30 TX with four bullets in the back of his head.

Perhaps the 1970s came to end in an unlikely spot: *le parking* of avenue Foch, under the cobblestones of bourgeois Paris? Perhaps 1984 was the real knell of the 1960s, the notorious year that that other Champ Libre author, George Orwell, had long ago underscored? As the .22 calibre rifle had taken potshots at Lebovici's head, Mitterrand's much-hailed socialist victory of 1980 looked glib and the conservative rot steadily set in everywhere. At the forefront were Ronald Reagan and Margaret Thatcher, who had perversely promised to fill the post-Keynesian emptiness; politics and economics would never be the same again.

Somewhere and somehow the Left had lost its way and welfare-state capitalism was all but moribund. Suddenly, Lebovici was as dead as French party-political socialism. In the 1970s Debord had made a loyal ally and now he'd lost one, the only comrade he'd never actually fallen out with. Their friendship had flourished throughout the Baader Meinhof and the Red Brigade years, amid the violence and the bombs. In the process, Debord had strayed from Paris's streets and almost made another movie. He'd hid behind Renaissance Italian ramparts and jousted windmills in Spain. He'd stayed gallant and translated poetry, dreamt of Gypsies and wisecracked in slang. He'd sensed death nearing and drank away his fears. And now Lebovici was gone, assassinated by culprits to this day still at large, another friend inexplicably killed by bullets. As the sirens flared and the fingers began to point, Debord stood accused, yet again.

5

I Am Not Somebody Who Corrects Himself

There are times when one should only use contempt with economy because of the large number of people who necessitate it

Chateaubriand, *Mémoires d'outre-tombe*

It had been a gruesome death, a bizarre murder, a ruthless hit. Was it an execution or an assassination, a botched robbery or a crime of passion? Maybe it was a deal gone sour or a settling of accounts? Paris's finest sallied forth, fumbling in the darkness, powerless against the imponderable, almost as clueless as their counterparts in Edgar Allan Poe's 'Murders in the Rue Morgue': 'confounded by the seeming absence of a motive . . . puzzled, too, by the seeming impossibility of reconciling the voices heard in contention'.[1] In fact, the cops only had one real lead: the name 'François', retrieved from a crumpled scrap of paper in Lebovici's pocket, scribbled alongside the words 'rue Vernet, 18h 45'. Earlier that day (Monday, 5 March), Lebovici had met another cinema producer, Jean-Louis Livi, to discuss a future project. They'd lunched together and were later in mid-conversation at Lebovici's office when, at around 5.30 p.m., the phone rang: a mysterious interlocutor compelled Lebovici suddenly to quit the office and cancel all remaining appointments. Nobody knows who was on the other end; all that surfaced nine hours later, in a subterranean parking lot, were those few words, Lebovici's last.

Many were interviewed and not a few aspersions cast; theories and conjectures abounded, yet little solid stuck. Paris's press, meanwhile, appeared to mimic that of Poe's day: 'Many individuals have been examined', Poe's fictional newspaper noted, 'in relation to this most extraordinary and frightful affair . . . but nothing whatever has transpired to throw light upon it.' Thus, *L'Humanité*, three days after the Lebovici bombshell: 'The hypotheses on the motive of death are even more numerous and diverse than the complex personality the victim presented himself.' And on 12 March, *Le Parisien libéré* reported:

> As the days unfold, [the police] discover a complex character – secret, many-sided, whose life entails enormous and strange twilight zones, where money, success after success, wealth and society soirées coexist in a bizarre cocktail with a pronounced taste for clandestine action and dangerous company.

In this latter regard, Debord entered the fracas; the authorities would interview him at the quai des Orfèvres almost while the corpse was still warm. He must have felt like Diego Rivera after Trotsky had an axe buried in his brain: devastated at the loss of a friend and comrade, appalled by the accusations of his culpability. Needless to say, the police found nothing on Champot's most notorious habitué, no incriminating evidence, *rien* to suggest he'd connived in the assassination of his ally and benefactor. At first, Debord ignored their slander and innuendo. For a while he followed Chateaubriand's maxim: he branded contempt with economy, mobilizing classic Joycean principles of dissent: 'silence, cunning and exile'. Then, in defence of his character and in memory of his late friend, he penned *Considérations sur l'assassinat de Gérard Lebovici*, putting the record straight, telling every hack critic to go to hell. (He would later sue *Le Journal du dimanche* for libel after implying his 'evil influence' was responsible for the producer's assassination. He would subsequently win the case for an undisclosed amount.)

Twenty years on, the case remains unsolved and largely forgotten. Lebovici's life read like a novel. He could have easily figured in any Raymond Chandler *noir* tale. Dressed in his *louche* raincoat, pacing the boulevards, he even looked like Humphrey Bogart. But he could also slip into a tux just as nonchalantly, hobnob with the elite in the Coupole, sip champagne and exert the Midas Touch wherever he went. He was rich and couldn't fail at anything; he was hated by the Left for his bourgeois pretensions, and loathed by the Right for his *gauchiste* sensibilities. In the early 1980s he'd also started to organize his own campaign against pirate videos, a growing and lucrative niche, increasingly threatening the movie business. For all this, and much more, Lebovici had innumerable enemies, each side of the political spectrum and everywhere in the business community, any one of whom could have pulled the trigger or hired somebody else to.

In the months prior to his murder, Lebovici had been working on a bizarre memoir, an honest presentation of his personality, revealing 'everything on the character'. What he bequeathed were rough handwritten jottings and preliminary sketches, together with a bundle of letters that assorted friends and associates had sent him between 1974 and 1984. Much of the latter bordered on hate mail, and resurfaced in a posthumous text, *Tout sur le personnage*, published by Editions Gérard Lebovici, the re-launched Champ Libre – minus its prince. In it, Lebovici comes over as a ruthless editor and producer, a hard-nosed businessman who takes no shit and expects a lot in return. It's clear he's mauled manuscripts, rejected proposals, ruined careers and not returned calls. He's variously cursed and graphically denounced: He's called a 'lout', 'bloody stupid', 'pitiable', even a 'neo-Nazi'. Some threaten legal action; others, like former friend and colleague, Gérard Guégan, indict Lebovici for refusing to publish Guégan's second novel, *Les Irréguliers*, because it wasn't sufficiently extreme. Guégan suspects Debord's hand somewhere, and, under his disruptive influence, suggests that Lebovici's Champ Libre will quickly demise into 'Chute Libre' (free fall).

More attacks objected to Lebovici's 'reckless' publication of *L'Instinct de mort*, the controversial autobiography of Jacques Mesrine, then France's most notorious criminal. Lebovici was as fascinated with Mesrine as he was with Debord. For Lebovici, the legendary gangster, revered by France's underworld as a latter-day Robin Hood, was a 'perfect symbol of liberty'.[2] Good-looking and charming, Mesrine was courteous and elegant, even while he murdered and robbed banks. He lapped up danger and risk, masterminding armed heists with utmost military precision. He was a genius of disguise, too, donning wigs and changing his appearance in seconds, slipping through police blocks and escaping from maximum-security prisons. On the inside, Mesrine wrote an exaggerated memoir, bragging about killings he may actually never have committed. The book was smuggled out of prison and published, amid uproar, by Lebovici's Champ Libre a few months before Mesrine came to trial in May 1978.

Several days after being sentenced to twenty years hard time, Mesrine and his accomplice, François Besse, in a dramatically staged escape, held up warders at gunpoint and climbed over the wall to freedom. They are still the only two men to make it out of Paris's dreaded La Santé penitentiary. Once outside, they lost little time robbing a Parisian casino and soon plotted a series of revenge kidnappings. One had to wonder whether Lebovici ever made this list himself, especially since the convict at large was demanding royalties! On 2 November 1979, though, Mesrine had outsmarted the cops once too often. After a tip-off, an unmarked van full of policemen moved ahead of Mesrine's BMW at traffic lights in Paris's porte de Clignancourt, riddling the car with bullets, leaving Mesrine and his dog dead and his girlfriend crippled for life. He'd been shot 20 times by police sharpshooters, in an execution-style killing, without warning or proper procedure; Mesrine, plainly, was too dangerous to have rights.

Meanwhile, Lebovici befriended Mesrine's daughter, Sabrina, whose name may have been on the lips of Lebovici's anonymous caller. Lebo took Sabrina under his wing and would later formalize guardianship. Whether Sabrina was involved in the shooting of her millionaire custodian will probably never be known, or whether the François in question was in fact Mesrine's sidekick, François Besse, the popularly recognized 'Public Enemy Number Two'. At 5 feet and a fraction over 100 pounds, 'le Petit François' had been scot-free for years, leading a Ronnie Biggs-style life in Tangiers. But in 1994 he was recognized and arrested outside a café terrace. In June 2002 he was put on trial for past crime and misdemeanours. Whilst in jail, *petit* François repented like *jeune* Raskolnikov, and learnt Latin and absorbed himself in philosophy. When the jury finally cast its verdict – 'eight-years in La Santé' – *Libération* (13 June 2002) described the sentence as 'mild'. Is *petit* François a killer harbouring a secret? Did he avenge his partner Jacques, liquidating the man who'd been messing with Public Enemy Number One's daughter? Perhaps François was a blackmailer and Lebovici refused to cough up? Or maybe, just maybe . . . the perpetrator was simply another François?

Lebovici was put to rest in Paris's Montparnasse Cemetery, where, on a tomb that is crumbling and seemingly forgotten, are, in fading script, stanzas from Guy's translation of Jorge Manrique:

What friend for his friends!
What a Lord!
What an enemy for the enemy!
What leader of the fearless!
What judgment for the wise! . . .
What lion!

Debord completed *Considérations sur l'assassinat de Gérard Lebovici* in January 1985, probably drafting it over the previous summer in

Gérard Lebovici's gravestone with Debord's inscription, Montparnasse cemetery.

Champot. It would have been a sad period: grief-stricken over a lost friend, badgered by the media, barraged by vitriol. He was often crippled with gout and plagued by insomnia, too. Acquaintances were visibly shocked at how bad 50-something Debord looked. Distant and detached, he took to the pen, and brandished it like a blade. 'In all', he noted near the beginning of *Considérations*,

> I don't believe I've read more than five or six true facts reported about me . . . and never two together. And these same facts were almost always taken out of context, and doctored and misrepresented by diverse errors, and interpreted with much malevo-

lence and nonsense. All the rest was simply invention . . . Never have so many false witnesses surrounded a man so obscure.[3]

What followed in *Considérations* was Debord's settling of scores, a crafted and crafty act of retribution, citing an array of press clippings only to rip them apart for their inaccuracy and stupidity. He said he'd learnt a lot about dishing out insults from experts, particularly from the Surrealists, and especially from Arthur Cravan. But the art of the insult, he said, must never be unfair, must never utilize rash denunciations. As such, Debord strikes at his polemical best: mocking and dry, measured and smart. Since he was dealing with an unseemly pile of garbage, 'I will evoke what has been said in a similarly disordered manner . . . I would do too much honour to my subject if I were to treat it orderly. I want to show that it is unworthy of such treatment.'[4] At one point, Debord even reminds a Parisian newspaper about French regional geography: Bellevue-la-Montagne, he informed, isn't in the Haute Savoie as they stated, but in the Auvergne!

No, he didn't know Jacques Mesrine, or any terrorists or killers. Yes, Gérard Lebovici 'had attachments to the Haute-Loire. I am pleased that he always felt at home there.'[5] The 'inconceivable manner', he said, in which these publications commented on the Lebovici affair 'has led me to the decision that none of my films will ever be shown again in France. This absence will be a more just homage.'[6] Debord concludes *Considérations sur l'assassinat de Gérard Lebovici* with words that smack of his own epigraph, ten years *avant la lettre*:

It is fine to have contributed to the indictment of the world. What other success do we merit? I do not think I am so 'enigmatic' . . . I even believe I am sometimes easy to understand. Not so long ago, at the start of a passion, a woman whom I spoke to about the brief period of exile we'd each known, said to me in that tone of generous abruptness which goes so well in Spain: 'But you, you have spent all your life in exile.' So I have had the pleasures of exile, as others have had the pains of submission. Gérard Lebovici was assassinated.[7]

One can't underplay the effect all this must have had on Debord's nerves and temperament: it was enough to drive anyone to drink and into self-imposed exile. Lebovici's death signalled the end of middle age, the beginning of the real end for Debord, the grey on grey of life grown old. He never really seemed to get over it and withdrew even more from the modern world.[8] Still, by his standards, the ensuing years would mark a prolific writing period. He'd whip off, in fast succession, a couple of brilliant books, *Commentaires sur La Société du Spectacle* (1988) and *Panégyrique* (1989). Despite everything, his analytical and poetic powers hadn't escaped him. If anything, they may have become more acute, more lyrical, even more accomplished.

On odd occasions, too, he could be spotted in old Paris, haunting its streets, dressed like an *auvergnat paysan*, with a copy of *Libération* under his arm (a newspaper he hated), furtively hunting in the shadows, bracing the chill breeze that came in off the Seine and slithered through the rue du Bac. And sometimes in midwinter nights, in the Square des Missions Etrangères, with an air of indignation and impudence, an owl would obstinately repeat his calls. Like Hegel's fabled bird of Minerva from *The Philosophy of Right*, Debord's truth would now only spread its wings with the falling of dusk. He and Alice ensconced themselves into an elegant apartment at 109 rue du Bac, in the smart 7th *arrondissement*, next door to a tranquil little public garden at the Square des Missions Etrangères, which thirty years before had been the scene of a daring nocturnal Lettrist *dérive*. 'Square des Missions Etrangères', wrote Michèle Bernstein in her *Potlatch* field-notes (14 and 26 January 1955), 'may be used for receiving visitors, for being

Debord's apartment building at 109 rue du Bac, Paris.

stormed by night, and for other psychogeographical purposes.'

Number 109 stands amid a handsome row of mid-nineteenth-century buildings near the Bon Marché department store, the quintessential *grand magasin* immortalized in Zola's 1883 novel *Au Bonheur des dames* ('ladies' paradise'). The fictional Octave Mouret, the brazen promoter and innovative owner of the *Bonheur* store, mimicked the equally brazen Aristide Boucicaut, the real-life *patron* of Bon Marché, whose drapery business began at a more humble site along rue du Bac in 1852. In 1869 Boucicaut commissioned Louis-Charles Boileau to rebuild the premises across the street; Gustave Eiffel lent a further hand in 1876 with another extension, replete with dazzling glass light-wells and iron catwalks and bridges.

The misnamed 'good value' giant has been growing ever since, into a wealthy corporate giant, a veritable cathedral of consumption, with around 2,700 square metres of retail space; right outside Debord's door, with spectacular irony.

On sunny afternoons, out of his front window, Debord would have seen the light reflecting off the scrubbed white walls of number 128 across the street, the Seminary of the Foreign Missions, inaugurated by Jacques-Bénigne Bossuet's sermon in 1663. Legend has it that in 1830 the Virgin Mary appeared four times at its chapel, always wearing a white silk dress, and always palpable to the same novice nun, Catherine Labouré. Devout Catholics today venerate the seat as St Catherine's shrine. Medallions, on sale at the chapel, commemorate the miracle.

Another devout Catholic and one of the founders of French romanticism, François-René Chateaubriand, lived next door to the seminary between 1838 and 1848, in a basement flat at number 120, at the Hôtel de Clermont-Tonnerre. (His courtyard backed out onto the Foreign Mission's own.) The celebrated classicist, statesman and adventurer wrote his *Mémoires d'outre-tombe* there and was laid to rest at the seminary's chapel. (He ended up in his native Saint-Malo, in a tomb that stands dramatically atop craggy rocks near the sea's edge.) Gambier's impressive stone bust of Chateaubriand dominates the shale path at the Square des Missions Etrangères opposite. In Chateaubriand's posthumous *Mémoires*, the final passage, dated November 1841, reads:

my window, which looks out to the west on the gardens of the Missions Etrangères, is open. It is six o'clock in the morning; I see the pale and enlarged moon looming over the spire of the Invalides, fully disclosed by the first golden ray of the Orient. One could say that the ancient world is finished, and the new commences. I see the glint of dawn whose sun I will not see rise. It will only live on in me as I sit down beside my grave, after

Gambier's bust of Chateaubriand, in the Square des Missions Etrangères, Paris.

which I will daringly go down, crucifix in hand, into eternity.[9]

Chateaubriand came to rue du Bac to retire. With his American voyages done, his squabbles with Napoleon and Louis-Philippe over, his royalist days and pains of exile behind him, he commenced drafting his memoirs. But the waves and winds and solitude of the Brittany coast were never far away in his imagination, even while he went in search of the North-west Passage and fell in love with America's native peoples, those 'noble savages' who stalked primeval forests. After that 1791 trip, Chateaubriand idolized the American wilderness, setting two romantic tales there, *Atala* (1801) and *René* (1802), vignettes that would figure prominently in his weightier *Genius of Christianity* (1802). *Atala*, Chateaubriand claimed, demonstrated 'the harmonies of the Christian religion with the scenes of nature and the passions of the human heart'; René, like Goethe's young Werther and Turgenev's Bazarov, showed the foolish dreams and fatal melancholy of impassioned love.

With his own voyages seemingly done, and his adventures likewise behind him, weeping over the death of Lebovici, Debord similarly retreated to his Mission at rue du Bac. As a canny urban physiognomist, he obviously knew Chateaubriand had lived opposite. From his building's front door, Debord would have been able to glimpse Gambier's stone bust. Was it accident or incident that brought him back so near to this stubborn Catholic romantic? Debord had studied Chateaubriand's work. He'd cited it approvingly in *Panégyrique*, itself a Catholic title filched from Bossuet, the seventeenth-century theologian: 'Chateaubriand pointed out – and rather precisely, all told: "Of the modern French authors of my time, I am also the only one whose life is true to his works."'[10] This same loyalty Debord could now privately savour, along with Alice, at the rue du Bac, drinking high-end Burgundy while listening to low-end cabaret.

At rue du Bac, he and Alice tuned into the old shanties of Pierre Mac Orlan, singing along to Germaine Montero's renderings of misty quays, sailors' bars, all-night dancing and mysterious women of the night. The prolific novelist and essayist Mac Orlan revelled, as Debord did, in the secret odour of the *demi-monde*, achieving fame in the 1920s for *Le Chant de l'equipage* (1920) and *Le Quai des Brumes* (1927). (The latter became Marcel Carné's *noir* classic starring Jean Gabin and Michèle Morgan as the worn dancehall belle Nelly.) In his youth, Mac Orlan was an intrepid traveller himself who had lived in turn-of-the-century Montmartre, hung out at Le Lapin agile and befriended Modigliani, Picasso and Apollinaire. He once interviewed Mussolini, had a mad passion for rugby – especially for the Le Havre Athletic Club – and somehow, along the way, wrote his famous ditties for the accordion. Germaine Montero, Juliette Gréco, Monique Morelli and Catherine Sauvage have all sung Mac Orlan's best titles.

Those songs, like Mac Orlan's stories, brim with comedy and mystery, and oscillate between the jocular and macabre. All of them somehow bask in the subtle ambiance he'd label *fantastique social*. 'Like there exists an adventurer', Mac Orlan had said, 'active without imagination and often insensible, all the less endowed with a feeling that escapes us, there are creative people in the shadow of the fantastic who themselves participate a little in the impressions of some privileged onlooker.'[11] These privileged participants became seminal 'passive adventurers', a category Mac Orlan made his own in a 1920 essay, *Petit manuel du parfait aventurier*. Passive adventurers stood in direct contrast to 'active adventurers', those young virile types, men of action who ran off with the Foreign Legion, joined the colonial infantry or set sail with the navy. Active adventurers explore to forget, to seek fortune, to find distraction. They desperately 'need to conquer', Mac Orlan thought. For the active adventurer, certain 'traits are essential: the total absence of imagination and feeling. He doesn't fear death because he can't explain it; but he fears those who are clearly stronger than him.'[12]

Passive adventurers, on the other hand, are more sensitive explorers, more cerebral, more studious and solitary, reading a lot and dreaming often. Passive adventuring, Mac Orlan maintained, is an art form, 'a question of intellectual gymnastics, understanding everyday exercises and practising the methodology of the imagination'. 'Like fetishism in the things around love, the passive adventurer applies his force to the mysteries of the personality of everyone.'[13] Voyages here are more commonplace, more carefully chosen: cities and cabarets, burlesque and books, wine and song, love and hate, intimacy and death. 'If I had to raise a statue of Captain Kidd', said Mac Orlan, 'I would put up at the foot of the monument the gentle and meditative figure of Robert Louis

Stevenson, the immortal author of *Treasure Island*.'[14]

Listening to Mac Orlan's songs, reading his books, studying Debord's life and following his trail, one could justifiably wonder: what kind of adventurer was Guy Debord? In a way, it's obvious, but only now can we state it: he was a preeminent passive adventurer. There's a telling moment in another Mac Orlan text, his novel *La Vénus internationale* (1923), in which Mathieu Raynold, a jaded publisher, remarks to his old friend Nicolas Gohelle: 'A man lives two existences. Until the age of 45 he absorbs the elements surrounding him. Then, all of a sudden, it's over; he doesn't absorb anything more. Thereafter he lives the duplicate of his first existence, and tries to tally the succeeding days with the rhythms and odours of his earlier active life.'[15] Perhaps Debord himself was now trying to negotiate these two existences, something he'd begun with *In Girum Nocte et Consumimur Igni* in 1978, a project he'd completed a little after his 45th birthday. Perhaps without knowing it, he was already retreating behind the high fortress wall in Champot, or to his sumptuous apartment at rue du Bac with the rhythms and odours of 1950s Paris, odours immutably inscribed in his imagination. In the past, Debord had been an 'active adventurer', a maverick voyager, somebody who'd actively sought out novelty and change. Later, he'd developed into a supreme Mac Orlanian 'passive adventurer', purposefully cutting himself off from anything real or active.

That's why Debord adored Mac Orlan: he let Debord glimpse himself in his own living room, at Champot, Arles, Florence or at the rue du Bac, where he could journey to distant shores, go to far-off urban spaces, make daring visitations, get drunk and dance, and still feel at home. And, like Debord, he could take you there with him. Debord's life was an active voyage of discovery – engaging in covert activities here, disturbing the peace there; and yet, for all that, his enduring legacy is perhaps how he tapped the mysteries of the urban unconscious, unearthed the sentimental city, opening up its everyday heights and illuminated its nocturnal depths. Mac

Orlan helped Debord retrace his steps through ruins and recapture an everyday sentimentality of an epoch of streets and hoodlums and cheap thrills. Alongside Mac Orlan, he understood not so much the promise of the future as the power of the past, a phantasmal zone that's almost gone but needs defending. 'It isn't', said Mac Orlan near the end his memoir *Montmartre*, 'for regretting the past that one needs to meditate on this detail, but for regretting the future.' 'Where are the kids of the street', Mac Orlan laments in *A Sainte-Savine*, one of his popular songs for the accordion, penny poems put to music that Debord knew so well, 'those little hoodlums of Paris/ Their adolescence busted/ By the prejudices of midnight?/ Where are the gals of Sainte-Savine/ Singing in dancehalls aglow?'

At rue du Bac, in the spring of 1988, Debord also put the finishing touches to *Commentaires sur la société du spectacle*, his admirable sequel to the 1967 original. Many people may then have thought that Debord was already dead, or that he'd disappeared into obscurity, gone underground somewhere, vanished into a black hole like his heroes Arthur Cravan, Lautréamont or François Villon. Moreover, two years after its publication the world had witnessed two incredible events that seemed to fly in the face of the book's brooding thesis. The first was the tearing down of the dreaded Berlin Wall, heralding the implosion of decades of tyranny; the other was Nelson Mandela's dramatic release from Robben prison after 20 years of incarceration. Each, in different ways, signified resounding victories for freedom and human rights, ushering in a dizzy optimism about a future that Debord deemed only bleak. Big changes could take place – indeed, they *had* happened. Things were really up for grabs, after all. At least it appeared so. The first chink in this optimism was the appearance of *The End of History* (1992) by Francis Fukyama, a Japanese-American conservative who had studied Hegelian philosophy in France.

It was hard to know whether Fukyama's epiphany came from the mighty German idealist or from the rambunctious Sex Pistols

lead: 'The end of history' sounded like the 'No future!' refrain
Johnny Rotten sang a decade previously, with irony and a dim
sense of hope. Fukyama's teleology was really an apologia for
free-market capitalism. For intellectual credibility, he loosely
appropriated Hegel's philosophy of history: conflictual and
contradictory history would cease, Hegel said, with the advent
of the liberal bourgeois state, the absolute ideal incarnate, which
would simultaneously recognize individual particularity within
institutional universality. In Hegel's shadow, Fukyama said history
had given other big ideals a chance: fascism during the 1930s,
communism after 1917. Both had been doomed alternatives,
Fukyama thought, now dispatched to the dustbin of history. Only
one idea stayed intact: liberal-bourgeois market democracy. Nothing
else mattered; no alternative could be brooked: history had stopped
dead in its tracks. It got no better than this; here we are, forever.

Not long after, this mentality reinforced itself with yet another
clarion call: 'TINA' – 'There is no alternative'; and then, hot on its
heels, came George Bush Senior's speech on the 'New World
Order'. (These mantras would soon congeal into a headier thesis:
globalization.) Once, history seemed to be opening up; now, everything perplexingly began to close down. Never had bright skies
been so fast occluded by storm clouds. Suddenly, under our noses
and before our very eyes, democracy was hijacked, usurped by free-
market Stalinism. Meanwhile, another strange thing was unfold-
ing: just when the Right was triumphant about its 'meta-narrative'
of the market, the Left started to proclaim its incredulity to all
meta-narratives, to all big stories about humanity and progress.
Soon they'd begin to proclaim a viewpoint called 'postmodern'.
One of its ablest commissars was an ex-'Socialism or Barbarism'
1960s activist, Jean-François Lyotard, who stressed the non-founda-
tional nature of truth. In our present 'post-industrial' society,
Lyotard said, partial pragmatic truths – those refracted through the
gaze of media lenses – are the best we can hope and struggle for.

Truth, he argued, becomes like storytelling; each tale is difficult to adjudicate, because everything has relative plausibility.

Thus the paradox: the Right had set off on its long march across the entire globe, dispatching its market missionaries, spreading TINA doctrines, cajoling here, oppressing there, using heavy artillery to smash anything in its path. At the same time, the Left had embarked on an intricate philosophical debate about the meaning of meaning. It was tough to know where to turn, or where to run. A lot of progressives embraced Lyotardian postmodernism or became besotted by deconstruction and post-structuralism. A few became Jacques Derrida groupies; others used clippers to shave off their hair, transforming themselves overnight into Michel Foucault lookalikes. Needless to say, Debord, the passé Marxist, the renowned drinker and metaphysician, the underground man of the Auvergne, was nowhere on anybody's radical radar. Notwithstanding, he'd unfashionably anticipated these comings back in 1988, well before they'd come to fruition.

His *Commentaires* on his earlier treatise were tinged with pathos and had a dark undertow. Yet his analytical scalpel hadn't blunted 21 years on, nor had his prose lost its clinical lustre or icy precision. And he was dead right. 'I am going to outline certain practical consequences', he warned,

> still little known, of the spectacle's rapid expansion over the last twenty years. I have no intention of entering into polemics on any aspect of this question; these are now too easy, and too useless. Nor will I try to convince. The present comments are not concerned with moralizing. They do not propose what is desirable, or merely preferable. They simply record what is.[16]

He expected his record to be welcomed by 50 or 60 people, 'a large number given the times in which we live and the gravity of the matters under discussion'.

Regrettably, says Debord, there will be too many things easily understood. The first is how rapidly the spectacle has grown in strength since the disturbances of 1968 and their failures to overthrow existing order. We thought it was bad enough in 1967. Now, the spectacle had spread to its furthest limits on every side, while increasing its density at the centre, learning new defensive strategies, as well as innovative powers of attack. Since *The Society of the Spectacle*, the society of the spectacle, with barely half a century behind it, has become ever more powerful, perfecting its media extravaganzas, raising a whole generation moulded by its laws. Ordinarily, Debord wasn't somebody who corrected himself.[17] Things, however, had deteriorated so palpably that they'd outstripped his darkest prognostications. History, accordingly, had forced him to intervene yet again. In different circumstances he'd have considered himself 'altogether satisfied with my first work on this subject, and left others to consider future developments. But in the present situation, it seemed unlikely that anyone else would do it.'

It's a tribute to Debord that *Comments on the Society of the Spectacle* was penned *before* the Berlin Wall was ripped down, *before* globalization – as an ideal and economic orthodoxy – was on every politicians' lips and in every free-marketeers' wet dream. The Wall had been the de facto demarcation between two rival forms of spectacular rule. On the eastern flank was a regime akin to what he'd formerly called the 'concentrated spectacle', with its ideology condensing around a dictatorial personality, whose mantle resulted from a 'totalitarian counter-revolution'. On the western flank emerged the 'diffuse spectacle', the Americanization of the world, driven by wage-earners applying 'freedom of choice' to purchase a dazzling array of consumer durables. The latter system was used to frighten many 'under-developed' countries; yet, more and more, it successfully seduced them to jump on the bandwagon.

With the Wall gone, the former Eastern bloc could now be seduced, too. Henceforth two hitherto separated spectacular forms came together into their 'rational combination': the integrated spectacle. 'It is this will to modernize and unify the spectacle', mused Debord in a 1992 preface to his original treatise, 'that led the Russian bureaucracy to suddenly convert, like a lone man, to the present *ideology* of democracy: that is to say, the dictatorial liberty of the market, tempered by the recognition of the Rights of Spectacular Man.'[18] 'Nobody in the West', Debord maintained, 'had for a single day held forth the significance and consequence of one so extraordinary media event.' By 1991 Russia had almost entirely collapsed, 'expressing itself more frankly than even the West, the disastrous general evolution of the economy'.[19]

When the spectacle was concentrated, 'the greater part of surrounding society escaped it; when diffuse, a small part; today, no part'. The integrated spectacle has now

> spread itself to the point where it permeates all reality. It was easy to predict in theory what has been quickly and universally demonstrated by practical experience of economic reason's relentless accomplishments: that the globalization of the false was also the falsification of the globe.[20]

Nothing is untainted anymore, nothing in culture or in nature; everything has had its halo torn off, its sentimental veil peeled back; everything has been 'polluted, according to the means and interests of modern industry. Even genetics has become readily available to the dominant social forces.'[21]

The integrated spectacle, Debord said prophetically, has sinister characteristics: incessant technological renewal; integration of the state and economy; generalized secrecy; unanswerable lies and an eternal present.[22] Gismos proliferate at unprecedented speeds; commodities outdate themselves almost every week; nobody can step down the same supermarket aisle twice. The commodity is beyond criticism; useless junk nobody really needs assumes a vital life force that everybody apparently wants. The state and economy have congealed into an undistinguishable unity, managed by spin-doctors, spin-doctored by managers. Everyone is at the mercy of the expert or the specialist, and the most useful expert is he who can lie best. Now, for the first time ever, 'no party or fraction of a party even tries to pretend that they wish to change anything significant'. Now, too, there can be no enemy of what exists. 'We have dispensed with that disturbing conception, which was dominant for over two hundred years, in which a society was open to criticism or transformation, reform or revolution.'

Without any real forum for dissent, public opinion has been silenced. Masked behind game shows, reality TV and CNN, news of what's genuinely important, of what's really changing, is seldom seen or heard. 'Generalized secrecy stands behind the spectacle, as the decisive complement of all it displays and, in the final analysis, as its most vital operation.' With consummate skill, the integrated spectacle thereby manufactures consent, 'organizes ignorance of what is about to happen and, immediately afterwards, the forgetting of whatever has nonetheless been understood'. Ineptitude compels not laughter, but universal respect. The present is all that matters. In fashion, in clothes, in music, everything has come to a halt: you must forget what came before, or else reinvent it as merchandise. Furthermore, it's no longer acceptable to believe in the future. 'The end of history', said Debord, pre-Fukyama, 'gives power a welcome break.' History has been outlawed, the recent past driven into hiding, the deep past a forgotten memory. The integrated spectacle covers its tracks, concealing the process of its recent conquests. 'Its power already seems familiar,' he said, 'as if it had always been there. All usurpers have shared this aim: to make us forget that *they have only just arrived.*'[23]

Our self-proclaimed democracy also constructs its own inconceivable foe: terrorists. 'Its wish is *to be judged by its enemies rather than by its results.*' Spectators must certainly never know everything about terrorism, 'but they must always know enough to convince them that, compared with terrorism, everything else must be acceptable'.[24] Every enemy of the spectacle is a terrorist enemy; all dissenters – grievances notwithstanding – are terrorists. Spectacular authorities need to infiltrate, compile dossiers and eliminate critique – authentic or not. Unexplained crimes are either suicides or terrorist attacks. Terrorists themselves soon feel the wrath of state terrorism: Mossad kills the Jihad in the Lebanon; the Contras do likewise with the Sandinistas in Nicaragua; ditto the SAS with the IRA in Northern Ireland; the GAL with ETA in Spain and the CIA with al Quaeda in Afghanistan. In this context, Mafiosi flourish: Colombian drugs Mafia, Sicilian Mafia, Fundamentalist Mafia, and of course White House Mafia. New forms of economic integration necessitate new bonds of dependency and protection. As such, the 'Mafia is not an outsider in this world; it is perfectly at home. Indeed, in the integrated spectacle it stands as the *model* of all advanced commercial enterprises.'[25]

On and on *Commentaires sur la société du spectacle* went, lashing out, venting spleen, waxing majestically, with bile. In many ways, it was an even angrier text than *Considérations sur l'assassinat de Gérard Lebovici*. It mercilessly indicted not actual newspapers or journalists, but the whole structure of society, our institutions and governments, all in cahoots together, all as pathological and deceitful as one another, all so in control that they're out of control. In 1984 Debord branded sarcasm and irony to avenge the death of his friend; in 1988 he gave the finger to the totality of modern political and economic life. He signs off not with a revolutionary call-to-arms, but with an enigmatic passage from Sardou's nineteenth-century *Nouveau dictionnaire des synonymes français*, ruminating on the meaning of the word *vain*. You sense this is some key, valedictory moment that Debord is sharing with us. It's a parable of a life of intrigue and lost battles, disguised in a single paragraph, intelligible for those who know. It has a beguiling poignancy, a recognition that he was right all along, and being right meant he won even when he lost. For, although his struggles had somehow been in vain, that didn't undermine the righteousness of the effort. Thus:

> one has worked *in vain* when one has done so without achieving the intended result, because of the defectiveness of the work. If I cannot succeed in completing a piece of work, I am working *vainly*; I am uselessly wasting my time and effort. If the work I have done does not have the result I was expecting, if I have not attained my goal, I have worked *in vain*; that is to say, I have done something useless . . . It is also said that someone has worked *vainly* when he has not been rewarded for his work, or when this work has not been approved; for in this case the worker has wasted time and effort, without this prejudicing in any way the value of his work, which indeed may be very good.

Less than a year after *Commentaires sur La Société du Spectacle*, Debord wrote another book, a romantic and poetic eulogy to himself. In 1988 he'd negated, had spoken of everything he hated about the modern world, everything we knew was true; in 1989, he affirmed, he spoke about everything he loved about life. Even staunch critics couldn't deny its literary brilliance and touching melancholy. *Panégyrique* supplanted pessimism with the joys of resistance and the pleasures of *resisting*. A leopard dies with his spots; so shall I, he vowed. He is what he is. In good times, he held no private interests; in desperate times, he feared nothing. 'History is inspiring', Debord recalled. 'If the best authors, taking part in its struggles, have proved less excellent in this regard than their writings, history, on the other hand, has never failed to find people who had the instinct for the happy turn of phrase to communicate its passions to us.'[26] During the Mexican Revolution, for instance, Francisco Villa's partisans sang: 'Of that famous Northern Division,/ only a few of us are left now,/ still crossing the mountains/ finding someone to fight wherever we go.'[27] We are, he said, woven of a cloth that's made to dream. He was a prime example of what his epoch didn't want. Forgive him his faults.

Panégyrique was Debord's literary grand finale. He'd never approach its eloquence again. He would publish his last real book, *Cette mauvaise réputation*, in 1993, duelling once more with the French media, who refused to let up sullying the ex-Situ's reputation. But penned when peripheral neuritis worsened, this was a bitter effort. Dante once said it is with a knife that the slandered should respond to such bestiality. They were different days, Debord laments. So he'll use instead the more modern method of parody and polemicism. Not having worked demanded great talent, he reminded his critics. 'I have never believed that anything in the world was done with the precise intention of pleasing me.'[28] Perhaps the most telling line in the book, written a year before his death, is this: 'I am not someone who could be drawn to suicide . . . by imbecilic calumnies.'[29] 'I hope', he said, citing Georgias de Léontium as the book's epigraph, 'to have held myself to this rule at the commencement of my discourse. I have attempted to annul the injustice of this bad reputation and the ignorance of opinion.'

One of the last things Debord wrote, three days before he took his own life, was a letter to the editor of a posthumous collection of 'contracts', agreements in which 'nothing is legal; and it is exactly this special form that renders them so honourable.' Debord said he'd had an idea for the cover of *Des contrats*:

> It's a card from Marseilles tarot, to my mind the most mysterious and finest: *the bateleur*. It seems to me that this card would add, without having to imply it too positively, something one would be able to see as a certain mastery of manipulation; and in recalling opportunely the full extent of his mystery.[30]

In *Des contrats'* preface, a knowing Debord voiced a Spanish proverb:

'We have only two days to live.' 'It is a principle', he added, 'naturally little favourable in financial speculation.'

Debord will always seem like a *bateleur*: a little mysterious, a little menacing, and a lot impish. In an odd way, the *bateleur* might be the great symbol of revolt and resistance in our day: allusive and playful, intelligent and full of tricks, at once an outsider and a court jester. In every sense, they're somebody *who knows* – a mythical medieval *voyou qui sait*. It's someone able to live both within and beyond the integrated spectacle, using conjuring skills to deceive and to search for lost and new wisdom. The *bateleur* belongs to the oldest and most popular tarot variant now in use. Nobody knows, for sure, how tarot came about. Gypsies, Jews, Sufis, Freemasons and assorted religious and esoteric groups all claim authorship. And tarot makes allusions to the Gospels and the Book of Revelation, as well as to Cabbalist, astrological and Tantric teachings. Out of this complex *mélange*, Marseilles tarot somehow emerged, whose first-card protagonist is the mysterious juggler/magician/trickster.

The *bateleur* signifies a beginning, somebody on the rise. For him, everything's possible and trickery is his practised *métier*. Like all magicians, by gestures and through speech, he creates a world of illusions. His hand tricks the eye; he thrives off ambivalence. In luring us toward his act, egging us nearer his conjurer's table, he invites us to go beyond appearances. He makes us feel uncomfortable. He looks and feels very strange and we're not sure if he's an impostor. But we know, too, that he might hold knowledge of secret essentials. He might possess the mysteries of unity that help us accomplish our destiny.

The classic image of the *bateleur*, adorning *Des Contrats* and every Marseilles tarot card, is of a young man with blond curly locks wearing bright tricoloured – red, blue and gold – minstrel's clothes. He looks sharp and cocky in his big floppy hat, standing in front of a wooden table, holding something red, perhaps a magic wand or a baton. On the table are various artefacts, elemental tools of his trade:

glasses, knives and coins. The glass represents thirst, whose key constituent is water, the symbol of knowledge; the knives signify swords, emblems of air, action and courage; the wand suggests a baguette, the image of primordial fire; and the coins are earthly material, evoking the land. The *bateleur* treads fearless along paths where your quest leads you. He never forgets that the grandest revolutions are made in peace and love. It's interesting, and not coincidental, that Debord wanted to bid *adieu* with an illustration of an image of creation and commencement. His farewell constitutes a debut, a possibility. That was his final spell, the last wave of his red wand.

The autumn of 1994 was particularly wet and dismal in the Haute-Loire. It poured for days on end. Damp seeped deep into the stone walls of every house and made things feel cold and unbecoming. Guests no longer visited Guy and Alice, and they spent quiet days and nights alone. He sipped wine slowly, read, smoked his pipe and played *Kriegspiel* while listening to rain dance off the roof and gush along the gutters. During his last months, Debord could hardly walk without his cane. He found getting in and out of the car difficult. Alice ran all the errands now, to Bellevue and Le Puy, to Saint-Paulien and Craponne. He rarely left the Champot Haut farmhouse. He'd refused to seek treatment in the early stages of illness; now it was too late, too futile. Nothing could be done. He'd refused to let up drinking, and the burning pain throughout his body worsened.

According to medical encyclopedias, peripheral neuritis or alcoholic polyneuritis is a disease caused by the toxic effects of alcohol on the nerve tissue. It's a drinker's ailment. It can lead to long-term chemical poisoning of the body, which inflames the outlying nerves and affects the muscles in the arms and legs. At first, there's a loss of sense of touch, then pins and needles, and, in more progressive cases, numbness and disability, as well as acute pain in joints and muscles. Insomnia and gout are not uncommon in an illness that seems to manifest itself as a cross between arthritis and multiple sclerosis. It's a malady that is treatable and, indeed, curable, if spotted early and if the patient takes mineral supplements and physical therapy, exercises and, above all, stops drinking.

Debord did none of this, of course. In fact, he did the exact opposite: he turned his life of drink into a form of lyrical poetry; his drinking problem became an oeuvre, a magnificent and terrible peace, writing some of the most prosaic passages of *Panégyrique* on the only thing, he said, he'd ever done with real aplomb.[31] 'There is what is drunk in the mornings', he wrote,

> and for a long while that was beer. In *Cannery Row* a character who one could tell was a connoisseur professes that 'there's nothing like that first taste of beer'. But I have often needed, at the moment of waking, Russian vodka. There is what is drunk with meals, and in the afternoons that stretch between them. There is wine some nights, along with spirits, and after that beer is pleasant again – for then beer makes one thirsty. There is what is drunk at the end of the night, at the moment when the day begins anew. It is understood that all this has left me very little time for writing, and that is exactly how it should be.[32]

He'd hidden his fame in taverns, but now his secret was out; he'd drunk one too many *coups* for the road.

Debord apparently owned several antique pistols and a Winchester rifle; any one of the former could have been used on himself, for the one fatal shot into his heart on that dreary afternoon on 30 November 1994. Did Alice know of his intention? It seems that she was complicit. It's difficult to imagine how she felt at the hour, and in the days preceding, the secret she guards today, the memory she retains of him, the noise of a single shot ringing out across the moors . . . 'Guy wasn't condemned', Alice said in a 1998 interview. 'He condemned himself.'[33] It's the story of his life in a single sentence, a life lived on his own terms, set to his rules, clues of which were given in his 1973 film version of *The Society of the Spectacle*. The scene is purloined from Orson Welles's 1955 movie *Mr Arkadin*, where the eponymous protagonist Gregory Arkadin, ruining himself as he stays true to his nature, relays the parable of the scorpion and the frog. The former wants the latter to carry him across a river he can't swim himself. But if I take you on my back, the incredulous frog enquires, you'll sting me and we'll drown together. Why would I do that, responds the scorpion, it's against my better interests. Halfway across he stings the frog, and, as they are both about to sink, the frog wonders: Logic? Where's the logic? I could do nothing else, says the scorpion, it's in my character. 'Let's drink to character!' Debord shows Arkadin toasting. 'Let's drink to friendship!'

Alcoholic polyneuritis was first spotted in the autumn of 1990. 'D'abord presque imperceptible, puis progressive. Devenue réellement pénible seulement à partir de la fin de novembre '94' stated Debord in a final letter, which he'd mail to Brigitte Cornand, to be included in a posthumous TV documentary, *Guy Debord, son art et son temps*. 'Comme dans toute maladie, on gagne beaucoup à ne pas chercher, ni accepter de se soigner. C'est le contraire de la maladie que l'on peut contracter par une regrettable imprudence. Il y faut au contraire la fidèle obstination de toute une vie.'[34] It was a typical Debordian refrain, majestic and undefeated to the bitter end, a leaf out of Manrique's *Coplas*: 'At first almost imperceptible, then progressive', he'd said.

It became really painful from the end of November 1994. As with all incurable illnesses, one gains a lot by not seeking to, nor accepting, to cure oneself. It is the opposite of an illness that one can contract by regrettable imprudence. One needs, on the contrary, the faithful obstinacy of an entire life.

6

Land of Storms

It was, first of all, a game, a conflict, a voyage.

Guy Debord, *In Girum Imus Nocte et Consumimur Igni*

Debord was cremated in Saint-Etienne, the nearest big town to Champot. A few days later, Alice and several close friends travelled up to Paris where, from the banks of the Square du Vert-Galant, toasting Guy's memory, she tossed his ashes into the Seine. The current carried his ashes downstream, towards some unknown tributary, out into a vast nameless ocean. Debord was floating downwind and downstream, and somehow he is taking others along with him, to places we can't foresee, can't predict. His spirit is there in all of them, even if his physical presence is absent.

A stone stairwell, reeking of piss and faeces, on Paris's oldest bridge, the Pont-Neuf, leads you down to the western tip of the Ile de la Cité. The square below, named after Henri IV's notorious gallantries, is really a narrow triangular outcrop, replete with a neat lawn that's shaped like the bow of a ship. At high water, it's often cut off from the rest of the Ile; at other times, you can walk through a concrete trench and access one of Paris's most tranquil and beautiful spots, a hidden oasis afloat on the Seine. The day Alice bid Guy farewell, rumour has it that a skull and crossbones was seen flying from some untraceable mast. At the square's entrance, a plaque commemorates Jacques de Molay, the Grand Master of the Order of the Temple, and a certain 'Guy', the mysterious

The Seine from the Square du Vert-Galant, where Debord's ashes were scattered.

commander of the Normandy Templars, both of whom were burnt alive there in 1314. (They were indicted for heresy by Pope Clement v; but at the stake protested their innocence. 'I should reveal the deception which has been practised and speak up for the truth', Jacques uttered. 'I declare, and must declare, that the Order is innocent. Its purity and saintliness is beyond question.')

Beyond the lawn is a cobblestone terrace with weeping willow trees that leads you to the water's edge. The Louvre dominates the Right Bank; aglow with sunlight it contrasts starkly with the muddy-brown Seine. Ahead, in the foreground, is the pedestrian walkway, the Pont des Arts, no doubt shimmering in the frosty air the day a tearful Alice returned Guy to where he really belonged: to Paris, to the river he'd so adored throughout his life. The tide of destruction and pollution, Debord said, had conquered the whole planet. So he could return to the ruins of Paris, since nothing better remained anywhere else. For a while, he'd enjoyed the pleasures of exile; now, he knew there is no exile. Nobody can hide in a unified world.

Several years into the new millennium, an epoch Debord never lived to witness, our world seems forever besieged by violent storms.

Weather fronts sweep in, destroy and move on increasingly swiftly, increasingly chaotically and unpredictably. History has never seemed so open, so unstable, so precariously teetering on the edge of a huge abyss: wars and terrorism, financial meltdown, ethnic cleansing, religious conflicts, class exploitations, epidemic diseases, irresponsible American imperial might. More than 1 billion people now scramble to make ends meet on less than a dollar a day. Meanwhile, the net worth of the world's 358 richest individuals equals the combined income of the world's poorest 45 per cent – some 2.3 billion people.

Super-state and supra-state authorities impose their will on the world's population, caretakering the common affairs of the global bourgeoisie, masterminding corporate bills of right and generally administering the integrated spectacle. Through assorted means they police and spearhead neo-liberal economic programmes everywhere. They both open up and seal off certain markets, lubricate free flows of capital and trade, and brandish big sticks over nation-states while promising an abundance of fresh carrots. Hence an ever-growing list of organizations and agreements, nostrums and acronyms: the International Monetary Fund (IMF), World Bank (WB), World Trade Organization (WTO), General Agreement of Tariffs and Trades (GATT), North Atlantic Free Trade Agreement (NAFTA), Free Trade Area of the Americas (FTAA), Multinational Agreement on Investment (MAI). Bizarrely, all have accompanied refrains celebrating the virtues of the free market: the clumsy fist of the invisible hand. In its grip, hyper-modern media spurs primitive accumulation of capital.

Standing at the Square du Vert-Galant, on the banks of the Seine, in 'old Europe', watching the river flowing, it's tough to ignore what's wrong with our new world. At the beginning of our quest for Debord we stood in front of a large stone wall, nosing against his Champot fortress. Now, at journey's end – at the place from where he departed – we watch the flowing river being driven by a relentless current. A wall is fixed and in your face, somewhere; a river is fluid and takes you elsewhere. Debord was a peculiar mix of each, both fixity and fluidity, a rock as well as a nomad, a defensive barrier and a perpetual gush of movement and imagination. He was, in Clausewitz's terms, a block of ice in the course of a river's flow; and yet, he was also a peripatetic wanderer, a river himself, whom nobody could step into twice. One implies stasis and preservation, the other movement and change. Clausewitz said the effectiveness of defence – the effectiveness of the fortress – hinged on two distinct elements, one passive, the other active. The latter, Clausewitz reckoned, couldn't be imagined without the former. Passive fortresses act as 'real barriers': they block roads, immobilize movement, dam rivers. Accordingly, they become 'oases in the desert', 'shields against enemy attack', 'buttresses for a whole system of defense'.[1]

In modern times, there's plenty that people around the world need to defend themselves against and to stay vigilant about. There's plenty that our present economic system wants to erase and colonize, wipe out and abuse, rip off and plunder, convert into some *abstract* space. 'Capitalist production', Debord told us in *The Society of the Spectacle*, 'has unified space, which is no more bound by external societies.'

> The accumulation of mass-produced commodities for the abstract space of the market, just as it has smashed all regional and legal barriers, and all corporative restrictions of the Middle Ages that maintained the *quality* of artisanal production, has also destroyed the autonomy and quality of places. This power of homogenization is the heavy artillery that brought down all Chinese Walls.[2]

Debord's sense of abstract space, like Marx's sense of abstract labour, embraces the law of value, the world of commodities, vast networks of banks, business centres, production entities, motorways, airports and information highways. And while big corporations hold the initiative in its production and consumption, abstract space somehow sweeps everybody along, moulding places and people in its logo, incorporating peripheries while peripheralizing centres, being at once deft and brutal, forging unity out of fragmentation.

As the tear gas has flowed, not on the boulevard Saint-Michel but on Seattle's streets, in Genoa, in Quebec, in Washington, in New York and elsewhere, and as cops wielding batons and water cannons have waded into young demonstrators, a re-energized militancy has generated steam. It's posed unflinching questions about our fragile democracy and corrupt economic system, and it's grappled for answers. It's shown an amazing capacity to politicize people, especially young people, those hitherto disgruntled with ballet-box posturing. Steadily, but surely, a kind of *new* New Left has congealed, perhaps into the first social movement of the new century. Debord never saw any of these battles and ransackings; but one wonders what he would have made of them. This time around the hairstyles and fashions of the protesters are different, and they speak in a different tongue and jostle a new-fangled enemy, like the World Bank, the IMF, the WTO, the Bush administration, multinational corporations. Notwithstanding, their spirit remains Situationist at heart: these activists want the world, and they want it *now*. Maybe this is one coastline where Debord's ashes have washed up, one beachhead of progressive defence and attack, a nearby shore where new oppositional vernaculars are spoken and new 'situations' re-enacted. He would have appreciated the play element of these new-wave protests. Their irreverent expression and gusto smacks of his Lettrist years and the early, idealist phases of the Situationists, when everything seemed possible and all was permitted. Then, as now, the politics of negation was a *game*. Then, as now, politics necessitated fun, meant creating a stir and kicking up a fuss; play nourished politics and political people were *Homo ludens*.

The idea harked back to Johan Huizinga, whose 1938 text bearing that stamp Debord had read during the 1950s. Huizinga and Debord agreed that the 'play element' was vital in human culture, always had been and always should be. In a 1955 commentary on Huizinga, made while still a Lettrist, Debord underscored the role of play in the journal *Potlatch*. In issue 20, he affirmed play as 'the only field, fraudulently restrained by the taboos in durable pretension, of real life'. In politics, in urban life, he said, 'it is a question now of converting the rules of play from an arbitrary convention into a moral foundation'.[3] Making play with the moral foundation of society underwrote Situationist politicking and mimicked Huizinga's reasoning from *Homo ludens*, who, almost twenty-years earlier, had asked:

> More and more the sad conclusion forces itself upon us that the play-element in culture has been on the wane ever since the 18th century, when it was in full flower. Civilization today is no longer played, and even where it still seems to play it is false play – I had almost said, it plays false, so that it becomes increasingly difficult to tell where play ends and non-play begins.[4]

In 2000 Americans averaged 1,979 hours on the job, an increase of 36 hours from 1990.[5] For a lot of workers, more labour is required simply to prop up their income. As purchasing power has declined and personal debt has burgeoned, people need to put in longer hours (and do more than one job) to buy what they feel they ought to have. Work, henceforth, has overwhelmed everything, absorbing free time, becoming a new belief system, a new deity. Unsurprisingly, little or no time exists for the family or leisure, and even less for civic duties and politics. For the 'lucky' ones, their company caters for every physical, psychological and emotional need. The corporate campus becomes 'a convivial cocoon', a 'workers' paradise, with child care, exercise facilities, cafés, therapists, grief counselors, laundries, post offices, bookstores, break rooms stocked with soft drinks and aspirin, and even a concierge service attending to special needs – such as ordering flowers'.[6]

The 'work-as-fun' mentality reinforces Huizinga's thesis on 'false play'. After all, work-as-fun justifies non-stop toil, dreaming of riches and stock options, of hot dot.com start-ups, where hippie 20-somethings play Frisbee *while* they put in eighteen-hour days. Meanwhile, bankers, stock analysts and overworked executives, on rare weekends off, pay real money to indulge in high-end recreation, ballooning and bungee jumping, scuba diving and skiing.

Maybe the Great Refusal means slowing down and opting out, laughing at the rules and engineering one's own festivals, one's own weekdays, as Debord had. The writing had been on the wall all along: *ne travaillez jamais!* Current street protest seems to be harnessing this energy, grabbing the moment and turning it into a situation. What the world needs more than ever are modern-day Don Quixotes and François Rabelaises, new romantic men and women from La Mancha, defiant dwellers of abbeys of Thélème, wise magicians of laughter and tears, humanists and utopians who reach for the stars because they want to stand upright. Play and laughter can become a revitalized seriousness, no joking matter, things essential and life-enhancing, not sidetracks and diversions to making money and accumulating commodities. Laughter can be therapeutic and political, with positive creative potentiality as well as negative critical power.

In the sixteenth century François Rabelais built a whole literary and philosophical edifice upon the positive aspects of laughter. His mockery of medieval authority can help us mock our own authority, our own contemporary seriousness and playing false, and restore a new sense of democracy, a new lighter meaning to life. In the bawdy and biting *Gargantua and Pantagruel*, with its great feasts of food and drink, and rambunctious revelling and coarse humour, Rabelais denounced medieval hypocrisy. 'Readers, friends', he warned his audience, old and modern alike, 'if you turn these pages/ Put your prejudice aside,/ For, really, there's nothing here that's contagious./ Nothing sick, or bad – or contagious./ Not that I sit here glowing with pride/ For my book: all you'll find is laughter: That's all the glory my heart is after,/ Seeing how sorrow eats you, defeats you./ I'd rather write about laughing than crying, / For laughter makes men human, and courageous.'

Debord himself was fascinated by medieval times and by wise-cracking free spirits; Alice keeps his fascination alive. 'Guy shared my interest in the Middle Ages', she admitted to me, *en plein air*, one late afternoon in July inside the Champot wall. 'He was enthusiastic about this work of mine and always encouraged it', she said, sipping red wine and puffing on her cigarillo. 'It's sad that he never saw me finish it.' He didn't live to see the final volume of her trilogy on slang and on the Middle Ages, *Du Jargon héritier en Bastardie*.

'This will be my last treatise on the subject', said Alice, 'it's over now, no more!' Johan Huizinga figured heavily in her concluding text. He'd once said that the medieval era exuded 'the ideal of the sublime life'. He said that the aspiration of attaining a pure and beautiful life, as expressed in the Middle Ages, sparked the notion of *chivalry*. This ideal of sublimity and chivalry, and the pursuit for a pure and beautiful life, still dramatizes Alice's personal and intellectual disposition, as it had always dramatized Guy's. It isn't so difficult to comprehend why Alice's feudal fascination persists. The Middle Ages internalized startling extremes; a sombre melancholy weighed on people's souls. Zealous religious piety coexisted with unrestrained corporeal indulgence; fierce judicial judgements with popular sympathy and laughter; dreadful crimes with tender acts of saintliness. Everyday life, in a nutshell, was brutal and immediate, raw and flamboyant.

Play became an antidote to totalitarianism, of whatever stripe. (Huizinga, remember, wrote as Hitler's darkness closed in, just as

Mikhail Bakhtin, that other prophet of play, wrote about Rabelais during the long nights of Stalin's purges.) Play flouted dogmatic norms and pilloried persecution. It set forth its own mores and created order. It also affirmed joy and embodied something profound. 'In play', said Huizinga, 'we may move below the level of the serious, as the child does; but we can also move above it – in the realm of the beautiful and the sacred.'[7] Alice concurred. 'Need we add again', she queried, at the close of *Du Jargon héritier en Bastardie*,

> to that which we'd stated in the preamble, that 'all play is first and foremost a *free* action . . . is liberty?' It appears the answer to this question is, yes. This, at any rate, is what the preceding pages have attempted to emphasize. The finest players having been those who, free until the very end, conducted a game in which they themselves fixed the rules, guided by this virtue so badly perceived nowadays: faithful, before all else, to oneself.[8]

Alice had galvanized the arena of play into the realm of language, into the secret codifications 'of those who know', know how to play, who expressed it in their covert speech, and who set their own terms of reference. Like play, life, she said, was really a game of chance, a roll of the dice, a conflict and a voyage, haphazard and open, a special language-game. The toughest and most honourable players make rules for themselves; and, in the course of their unpredictable lives, stick by them, always. Her late husband's spirit surely isn't very far away. Indeed, Alice reminds us, borrowing as a last word his Situationist catchphrase from *In Girum Imus Nocte et Consumimur Igni*: 'it was, first of all, a game, a conflict, a voyage.'

Alice had come full circle, after going around and around in the night, utilizing her own linguistic palindrome. She'd begun with Guy and ends with Guy. She was visibly saddened that he was no longer around to share it. The voyage was over, she hinted, and now we must begin again at the beginning. 'The idea of a voyage was something crucial for Guy', Alice told me. He'd seen it the way Gypsies do: not so much experiential as *ontological*. It's not that Gypsies necessarily voyage from place to place as they *are* voyagers; the voyage is *immanent* in who they are, in what they do, irrespective of whether they travel or not. Guy had similarly understood life as an ontological voyage. Time moves on, ineluctably, and people are consumed by fire. In *In Girum*, he'd signified the voyage through water and fire, through linear movement and punctuated passageways.[9] Water is temporal, healing and unrelenting, with no stepping in it twice; fire is combustible, about love and passion and the Devil. Fire illuminates the night, ignites the spirit; yet water can dowse the flames, extinguishes the charge. Together, they beget the current of life as well as the path toward death . . . 'All Guy's favourite poets dealt with the finite aspect of time', Alice said, 'with its slipping away, with the fragility of life: Li Po, Omar Khayyám, and Jorge Manrique.'

Alice presented me with a copy of her latest book, *Là s'en vont les seigneuries*, whose title is a verse from her late husband's translation of Jorge Manrique. 'There are rivers, our lives', Alice's last sentence reads, 'that descend towards the sea of death. There go the lordships themselves.'[10] *Là s'en vont les seigneuries* is less a book than a long essay introducing a dozen richly evocative, sepia-toned photographs of a lost Spanish Atlantis, the village of Rello, in ancient Castile. These images offer various perspectives on an almost-abandoned medieval fortress (population of eighteen), whose walls are crumbling into dust, dissipating with the wear and tear of time. They conjure up a now-defunct Spain, one of El Cid and Don Quixote, of arid plains and sweeping vistas, of old knights and cavernous silences, of odours of lavender and thyme.

Ruins seem to fascinate Alice as much as they fascinated Guy. 'He' and 'she' (as they're labelled in the text) visited Rello back in 1970. And Alice presents her most tender memoir to date on her late husband, a touching travelogue of that visit in which they sleep together in a tiny earthy room, scoff cheap *tortilla* and *tapas*, and drink vintage Rioja with comrades, 'toasting France, Spain and friendship'.[11] 'Never will we drink so young', says Alice, appropriating Guy's stanza from *In Girum*. 'In the sky, at night, amongst the stars, you will find me again', she signs off. *Hasta siempre, Amor.* Medieval fortresses are scattered everywhere around Champot, too. One, at Polignac, a 20-minute car ride south-east from chez Debord, with its stark eleventh-century ramparts, even looks like Rello. Formerly the cradle of one of France's grandest families, Polignac is similarly decaying, equally drifting away and eerily passé. Its fortress design, typical of a bellicose era when autocratic lords pitted themselves against one another, has as its pinnacle a fourteenth-century 32 metres high keep, sitting atop a great bulging outcrop of rock that's visible from miles in the distance.

> But where are the snows of bygone years?
> Prince, do not ask in a week
> Or yet in a year where they are;
> I could only give this refrain:
> But where are the snows of bygone years?
> . . . I must stop talking like this;
> the world is only illusion.
> No one stands up against death,
> Nor staves off its approach.
> . . . Where is Guesclin, the good Breton knight,
> or Dauphin, Count of Auvergne,
> and the late brave Duke d'Alençon?
> But where is the bold Charlemagne?

Within Polignac's mighty walls, medieval knights and crafty *bateleur*s found safety. Within Champot's mighty ramparts other crafty *bateleur* likewise found cover. Indeed, Champot felt like a passive adventurer's Camelot, self-contained, warm and safe. The wall seemed even taller from inside, even more robust and cut-off from reality, because somehow the garden is sunken below the level of the outside path. 'Guy loved the wall', Alice confessed. He'd employed a local mason to heighten it.

> It was the thing he liked most about the house. When we first summered here in the 1970s, Guy never thought he could live in the country. After all, he was a man of the streets and cities. But slowly he adjusted and grew to love the house, with its peace and its wall. He would look forward to coming. He would always be reading here . . . Guy read all the time.

The house, and the house next door, were both owned by her brother, Eugène Becker-Ho. As an ensemble, the houses had once been 'the Debord colony' – as some locals termed it. Debord once described the house as 'opening directly onto the Milky Way'; now, Alice herself had immortalized this in her poem 'Voie lactée'. She said Guy would go out at night, stand on the grass, and look up at the stars. 'He loved looking up at the Milky Way; he'd watch it for hours. But for me it was just too vast. It made me feel vertiginous. The poem I wrote was a very personal thing': 'the stars that so fascinated you/ Alone/ At night', but which made me 'feel dizzy'. With 'Raised eyes/ You found there/ Peace/ And Serenity.'[12]

It's here, within Champot's peace and serenity, that Debord also savoured classic Pierre Mac Orlan lines like: 'There exist a certain number of cities of adventure . . . The name of these cities brings an evocative precision to the spirit of passive adventurers.' 'One never should forget', Mac Orlan said elsewhere in *Petit manuel du parfait aventurier*, 'that adventure is in the imagination of those who desire it. It is effaced when one believes they've found it, and when one holds it, it's not worth looking at.'[13]

'Ah yes, Guy loved that Mac Orlan book,' Alice said, matter-of-factly. 'He'd read it many times over, knew it well. He adored Pierre

Mac Orlan.' Another of Guy's favourite Mac Orlan texts, Alice informed me, was *Villes*. A charming memoir of Mac Orlan's vagabond years between 1899 and 1927, *Villes* is a typical mixture of rhetoric and reality, evoking wandering and seaports, grubby back streets and shady, twilight characters, all of which hark back to another age, to a sentimental education seldom found on any latter-day curriculum. Mac Orlan's voice resonates with a rich tonality of innocence. This is a writer's adventure story: turning its pages kindles the imagination like the chance turning of an unknown street corner. Nocturnal street corners wend and weft their way through *Villes*. As we leaf through its time-served pages, beat-up personalities and nettle-ridden paving stones invade our living rooms and possess our minds. Suddenly, somehow, we find ourselves foisted backwards to *fin-de-siècle* Montmartre, outside the Lapin Agile tavern, sauntering along the rue Saint-Vincent in summertime, or loitering in winter at the place du Tertre, feeling its icy chill penetrate our threadbare overcoat and under-nourished body.

In *Villes*, we wander melancholically a step behind Mac Orlan's shadowy presence, a journey an ageing Debord made many times, penetrating Mac Orlan's enchanting urban labyrinth, a cascading array of back alleys and mangled memories, of wounded warriors and warped waysides. The narrative drift seems factual but the driving force is Mac Orlan's own *noblesse de phrase*. He showed Debord how to access the city of dream, the sentimental city, a city that all true urbanists hold in their hearts, come what may. 'Misery in Naples, in London, in Hamburg, in Berlin, in Paris, in Barcelona, in Anvers', Mac Orlan said,

> reveals itself through intimate details profoundly imprinted on memory. It's relatively easy to be stirred and to write about a city after having touched the picturesque of its neighbourhoods. Tragedy often mingles with the familiar odours of the street. Misery plunges everybody and everything into an infinitely

mysterious mist that permits the imagination to create literary characters more living than the living themselves.[14]

The shutters at Champot are open every July, August and September when Alice returns to the farmhouse. She cuts the grass and, for her, Guy still lives on in the balmy summer air. He's in her as well, and she's immortalized him in her poetry. In *D'Azur au triangle vidé de sable*, Alice evokes their singular presence:

> Our two halves only made one
> You are gone
> One half of me survived you
> When one half of you
> Stayed here in me
> If two only makes one
> By what subtle arithmetic
> *The Prince of Division*
> Had you the right
> to get the better of what was unique.[15]

In another touching, reflective stanza, 'De part et d'autre de cette arme', Alice says:

> You are the true woman of a hoodlum
> On either side of his arm
> We will have no more of our time
> We will see each other again I know not where
> . . . His face forever so sweet
> The memories are for tomorrow
> We will see again our *Indian*.[16]

Elsewhere, in 'Au centre de l'étoile flamboyante', Guy is a shining light and her guiding star: 'Written at the center of a *Flamboyant*

Star/ The letter 'ɢ'/ Appeared so brilliant/ to guide the protégée.'
At frailer moments, though, without his physical presence, Alice
admits:

I am afraid
Afraid of fear
. . . I am afraid of the night
And afraid of the day which follows
Afraid of love
And afraid of life without him
. . . And afraid of silence
Afraid of understanding
And afraid to see
Afraid of me
Afraid of others
Afraid of being me
And of not being me
Afraid of everything
Afraid of nothing
Afraid of being afraid
When it inhabits me
When it leaves me
I am afraid.[17]

Debord spent many evenings staring at the radiant night sky above
Champot's living planetarium. Millions of pearl-white stars twin-
kled brilliantly against a backdrop of deep infinite blackness, only
to be extinguished by a passing mist a moment later. It was a land
of storms. Storms have battered that pale stone wall surrounding
his house for a long while. But the wall has absorbed anything pelted
at it, and it's stayed upright and undaunted. Storms have also rained
down on the Seine, sometimes flooding the Square du Vert-Galant,
cutting it off temporarily from mainland Paris. Storms in Champot

and storms in Paris are two Debordian motifs that endure most: the stubborn older man in his fortress and the young voyager with his Argonauts. Searching for Debord meant scaling the former while swimming in the latter, peering over the wall while thrashing about against the current. Developing a head for heights and holding one's breadth in chopping seas, not swallowing too much salt water, helps you get a little nearer to Guy, to the man and mortal, to the thinker and his ghost, to the activist and archivist, to his work and legacy.

Despite how much Alice tries to deny Guy's legacy – there is no Debord legacy, she insisted, in a letter to *Le Monde* (1 November 1996) – his legacy is surely that he taught us how to follow Hegel's wonderful proclamation: 'to look the negative in the face and live with it'.[18] Living with the negative, Hegel said, is 'the magical power' that gives people *Being*, that brings meaning and definition to their lives, underwrites life as a voyage, as a quest. It is a weirdly positive force, entering through the back door, or flowing as an undertow. Debord spent a lifetime living with the negative, knowing its magical power. The power he leaves us today is the power to say No: to look the negative in the face and live with it forever. Of course, it may mean living with this negative *in vain*, never actually winning, never overcoming, never finding positive transcendence. Still, that doesn't prejudice the value of the work, which may indeed be very good. Nor does it preclude that in striving, in battling against the negative, we can discover for ourselves a truly authentic life.

Perhaps, then, the real legacy of Debord isn't so much his Situationist muck-raking as the more personal, stoical lesson he can teach us about how to stay true to our nature in these desperate times. In the late 1980s Debord expressed to the writer Morgan Sportès his admiration of Louis Malle's 1981 film *My Dinner with André*, a quiet set-piece about two playwrights, Wallace Shawn and André Gregory, rendezvousing for the first time in years at an old-moneyed New York restaurant. Christophe Bourseiller's *Vie et mort de Guy Debord* recalls Debord's numerous meetings with Sportès in assorted Parisian bars that Debord had chosen.[19] A good few have since closed their doors or else gone upscale; others, like Le Vin des Rues at 21 rue Boulard, just south of Montparnasse Cemetery, we can still imagine Debord frequenting, sitting furtively out of sight, reading Mac Orlan's *Les dés pipés*. 'He was a man from another century', Sportès said, 'like a feudal lord'. Their conversations rarely touched upon politics; Debord spoke only about art, film and literature. To Sportès he confessed a fondness for Robert Musil's *Man Without Qualities* and a disdain for Proust.

Malle's *My Dinner with André* might really be a glimpse of 'My Dinner with Guy'. Debord himself, after all, wasn't averse to organizing grand meals for his guests at Champot, where, 'at the banquet of life', he'd hold court around its large rustic wooden table, the centrepiece of the house. In *My Dinner with André* nothing much happens: its *form* is a kind of anti-cinema that Debord loved. There is no action, no music, no gimmicks – a couple of hours slowly unfold; two men (both of whom retain their real names) sit at table, eat an expensive meal and talk about what they've done over the past two years. 'Wally' Shawn, who wrote the screenplay along with André Gregory, dreads meeting André, the once-famous experimental playwright, but accepts the invitation nonetheless. André, we hear, helped Wally get his first theatre break, though since then André has opted out of the limelight, taking off on mystical adventures to Tibet, India and deserted Polish forests. Everybody believes he's cracked up and gone mad, and Wally presents him as a cranky freak. The dialogue starts off lightly, even whimsically, but then steadily the intensity and gravity get racketed-up; it's André's existential voyage that dominates; he could talk all day and night if need be. Wally, the realist and sceptic, worries more about paying his next rent demand. André, on the other hand, has been searching for new principles, for new meaning; his days of performing and pretending on stage – on the stage of real life – in a drama where he hasn't scripted either rules or dialogue, is done.

André is a probing man of the *anti*-spectacle, a raconteur who expresses the *content* of a mature Debordian politics. He bemoans the modern world's incapacity to feel anymore, overwhelmed as it is by electric blankets, central heating and air conditioning. People no longer have time to think, no longer want to think – are no longer allowed to think. He speaks of alienation like the young Marx. At one point, André even sounds like a young Situ: 'We're bored, we're all bored; we've turned into robots.' 'But has it ever occurred to you, Wally,' he confronts his incredulous friend, 'that the process which creates this boredom that we see in the world now may very well be a self-perpetuating unconscious form of brainwashing created by a world totalitarian government based on money?' 'Somebody who is bored is asleep,' André follows up, 'and somebody who's asleep will not say NO!'[20] As far as he's concerned, the 1960s were

> the last burst of the human being before he was extinguished. And that this is the beginning of the rest of the future . . . and that from now on there will simply be all these robots walking around, feeling nothing, thinking nothing. And there will be almost nothing left to remind them that there once was a species called a human being, with feelings and thoughts . . . and history and memory.[21]

But as darkness closes in, and as peoples' lives become dominated by the society of spectacle – 'the guardian of sleep' – there will be others, like André, like Guy, who'll see things differently, who will try to reconstruct a new future for the world, invent 'new pockets of light', as André calls them. They will resist by 'creating a new kind of school or a new kind of monastery', a new kind of 'reserve' – islands of safety where history can be remembered and the human being can continue to function, in order to maintain the species through a Dark Age. In other words, André insists, 'we're talking about an underground, which did exist during the Dark Ages in a different way . . . And the purpose of this underground is to find out how to preserve the culture. How to keep things living.'[22]

You get the sense that Debord saw Champot as a new kind of reserve, as a new kind of monastery, where he preserved the culture in an underground. It's there that he conceived what André called

> a new language, a new language of the heart . . . a new kind of poetry, that is the poetry of the dancing bee, that tells us where the honey is. And I think that in order to create that language we're going to have to learn how you can go through a looking-glass into a new kind of perception, in which you have that sense of being united to all things, and suddenly you understand everything.[23]

I can see in my mind's eye Guy nodding approvingly as he watched *My Dinner with André*, understanding what André meant when he said that we've got to find a way 'to cut out the noise, to stop performing, and to listen to what's inside', before it's too late. One wonders, as Guy had wondered, whether it's too late for most people, whether there's anything left of the collective project he'd helped hatch during the 1960s? Or whether, in fact, that mission to change the world now had to begin again by creating new undergrounds, and that they'd commence from within, a little closer to home, where you'd fight, as Debord cited Jorge Manrique saying centuries earlier, 'for your true king', 'the one you've created yourself'.

While the Guy Debord that can help us survive the beginning of the century is found on the other side of the Champot wall, it's fitting that he finally ended up in Paris, and in the Seine. Alice knew his Paris, his old Parisian urbanism, had been done over. But even in death the city still stood for something irresistible – still, in spite of it all, stood for hope, retained glimmers of light amid the setting sun. It was never a completely done deal. Even the showcase Left Bank retained its Left mountebanks. Like all big cities, Paris had an endless capacity to absorb and adapt to all thrown at it, and to somehow live on. Alice knew that, and wanted Guy back, back to Paris: she wanted him looking the negative in the face and dying with it. Paris was in him, in his bones, and it always would be. It once nourished his spirit and stimulated his brain; now it could re-energize his body, bring it to life again, perhaps seven leagues from this land, or maybe only a few steps away. In Paris, he'd found his zone of perdition; that memory lingered and could never be effaced nor denied.

This spirit can help us script our own lives. In searching for Debord we can find ourselves, become shipwrecked pirates who've found an island paradise, our bounty after the mutiny. Debord's presence will endure as the Seine endures, as it keeps on flowing: nobody can stop it. The fabled river of poetry and romance circulated through him in much the same way that Dublin's Liffey did James Joyce: no matter where Guy went, whether to Champot or Arles, to Florence or Barcelona, his big hometown vein kept on pumping. For Debord, as well as for the Joyce of *Finnegans Wake*, the 'Sein annews': it was Guy's sinew as well as the core of his Being, his 'Sein'. At the same time, the Seine 'anews', is eternally recurring and constantly renewing. So, on the banks of the Square du Vert-Galant, in our land of storms, we can stare out to sea one last time, thinking about Debord's past and our future, looking for his Situationist pirate ship on the horizon somewhere ahead. To begin again at the beginning, he'd said in *In Girum Imus Nocte et Consumimur Igni*. We go around and around and are consumed by fire. A way a lone a last a loved a long the riverrun, from swerve of shore to bend of bay . . .

References

1 Eyes for Blowing up Bridges

1 This is the list that Debord himself compiled in *Considérations sur l'assassinat de Gérard Lebovici* (Paris, 1993), pp. 87–8.
2 Ibid., p. 92.
3 Carl von Clausewitz, *On War* (New York, 1993), p. 471. The section entitled 'Fortresses' comes from Book 6, chapter 10.
4 Guy Debord, *Panegyric*, vol. i, trans. James Brook (London, 1991), p. 64; *Panégyrique*, vol. i (Paris, 1993), p. 70.
5 Debord, *Considérations*, p. 69.
6 Debord, *Panegyric*, vol. i, p. 6; and *Panégyrique*, vol. i, p. 15.
7 Debord, *Panegyric*, vol. i, p. 34; *Panégyrique*, vol. i, p. 42.
8 In a letter to Patrick Straram, dated 31 October 1960, Debord wrote: 'I had the occasion, and the time, to reread it [*Under the Volcano*] entirely, toward the beginning of September, on a train between Munich and Gênes. I had found it more fine, and more intelligent, than in 1953, despite loving it a lot then' (Guy Debord, *Correspondance*, vol. ii: *Septembre 1960–décembre 1964*, Paris, 2001, p. 40).
9 Malcolm Lowry, *Under the Volcano* (New York, 1971), p. 86.
10 Ibid., p. 50.
11 Debord, *Panegyric*, vol. i, p. 37; *Panégyrique*, vol. i, p. 46.
12 Debord, *Panegyric*, vol. i, pp. 48–9; *Panégyrique*, vol. i, pp. 56–7.
13 DST, or La Direction de la Surveillance du Territoire, established by de Gaulle in 1944 after Liberation from the Nazis, is France's equivalent to the CIA and MI6.
14 See Debord, *Considérations*, p. 67. In French, it is possible to pun both, since *mouches* means flies and *mouchards* police stool pigeons.

15 Debord, *Panegyric*, vol. I, p. 13; *Panégyrique*, vol. I, p. 24.

16 Debord, *Considérations*, pp. 77–78.

17 Debord, *Panegyric*, vol. I, p. 14; *Panégyrique*, vol. I, p. 26.

18 Debord, *Panegyric*, vol. I, p. 13; *Panégyrique*, vol. I, p. 24.

19 Debord, *Panegyric*, vol. I, p. 16; *Panégyrique*, vol. I, pp. 28–9.

20 *Détournement* is a word used in relatively common parlance in France. Its accepted meaning is 'reversal', 're-routing', 'diverting', even 'hijacking' – as in 'un détournement d'avion'. The Situationists appropriated the notion in its everyday understanding, yet gave it their own inflection, their own twisted meaning. Situationist *détournements* were literary as well as practical, urbanistic as well as political, inverting art and daily life simultaneously, pillorying it, devaluing accepted meaning and behaviour. *Détournement* would invent new values and different meanings, meanings that the Situationists believed to be creative preludes of the future.

21 *Les Chants de Maldoror*, in Lautréamont, *Oeuvres complètes* (Paris, 1946), p. 289.

22 Ibid., p. 292.

23 Ibid., pp. 251, 306, 251.

24 *Poésies*, in Lautréamont, *Oeuvres complètes*, p. 365.

25 Hervé Falcou kept all young Guy's letters. Fifty-five years later, on the tenth anniversary of Debord's death, they surfaced, beautifully reproduced in large-format colour facsimile. See Guy Debord, *Le Marquis de Sade a des yeux de fille* (Paris, 2004).

26 Arthur Cravan, *Oeuvres: poèmes, articles, lettres* (Paris, 1987), p. 107. See, too, Andy Merrifield, 'The Provocations of Arthur Cravan', *Brooklyn Rail* (June 2004).

27 Debord, *Considérations*, p. 35.

28 Breton's essay is included in Cravan, *Oeuvres*. This citation appears on p. 105.

29 See Debord to Alex Trocchi, 1 June 1959, in Guy Debord, *Correspondance*, vol. I: *Juin 1957–août 1960* (Paris, 1999), p. 233.

30 Debord, *Panegyric*, vol. I, pp. 43–4; *Panégyrique*, vol. I, p. 50.

31 Debord, *Comments on the Society of the Spectacle*, trans. Malcolm Imrie (London, 1990), p. 78; see *Commentaires sur 'La Société du spectacle'* (Paris, 1992), pp. 104–5.

32 Debord, *Panegyric*, vol. I, p. 23; *Panégyrique*, vol. I, p. 33.

33 The English translation unfortunately loses the wit of Debord's original phrase 'entrepreneurs de demolition'.

34 Guy Debord, *Mémoires, 1952–1953* (Paris, 1993).

35 Guy Debord, 'Introduction to a Critique of Urban Geography' (1955) in *Situationist International Anthology*, ed. and trans. Ken Knabb (Berkeley, CA, 1989), p. 5.

36 'Encore un effort si vous voulez être Situationnistes', *Potlatch*, 29 (5 November 1957); reprinted in *Guy Debord présente Potlatch, 1954–1957* (Paris, 1996), p. 277. In *Potlatch*, 30, Debord described the journal as an 'instrument of propaganda' and 'probably in its time the most extreme expression, which is to say, the most advanced search, for a new culture and a new life' (*Potlatch*, 30, in ibid., p. 282).

37 'Hurlements en faveur de Sade', in Guy Debord, *Oeuvres cinématographiques complètes, 1952–78* (Paris, 1994), p. 11.

38 Debord, 'Le Rôle de Godard' in *Internationale Situationniste* (Paris, 1997), p. 470.

39 'Hurlements en faveur de Sade', in Debord, *Oeuvres cinématographiques complètes*, p. 12.

40 Ibid., pp. 12, 17–18.

41 'A la porte', in *Guy Debord présente Potlatch*, p. 21.

42 'L'Architecture et le jeu', in ibid., pp. 155–8.

43 Johan Huizinga, *Homo Ludens: A Study of the Play Element in Culture* (Boston, MA, 1955), p. 9.

44 Ibid., p. 89.

45 Debord, 'Sur le passage de quelques personnes à travers une assez courte unité de temps', in *Oeuvres cinématographiques complètes*, p. 21.

46 Ibid., p. 31.

47 Debord defined psychogeography as the 'study of the precise effects of the geographical environment, consciously developed or not, acting directly on the affective behavior of individuals' (see 'Définitions' in *Internationale Situationniste*, p. 13).

48 'Interview: Henri Lefebvre on the Situationist International', *October*, 79 (Winter 1997), p. 80.

49 Ibid.

50 Henri Lefebvre, *Critique of Everyday Life: Volume One* (London, 1991), p. 202.

51 Now in his seventies, the anarchist rebel Vaneigem keeps going strong

in Belgium, where he resembles a latter-day Charles Fourier. His book of 1967, *Traité de savoir-vivre à l'usage des jeunes generations*, was recently republished in Paris. Vaneigem's text would be more widely known today if it hadn't been released the same year as *The Society of the Spectacle*, which became the radical book of the epoch.

52 Lefebvre, 'Interview'.

2 The Café of Lost Youth

1 Ralph Rumney, *The Consul* (San Francisco, 2002), p. 21.

2 Guy Debord, 'In Girum Imus Nocte et Consumimur Igni', in *Oeuvres cinématographiques complètes, 1952–78* (Paris, 1994), p. 223.

3 Ibid., pp. 223–5.

4 Ibid., p. 230

5 Jean-Michel Mension, *The Tribe* (San Francisco, 2001), pp. 38–3.

6 Ibid., p. 122.

7 Ibid., p. 41.

8 Ibid., p. 47.

9 Ibid., p. 51.

10 'Interview: Henri Lefebvre on the Situationist International', *October, 79* (Winter 1997), pp. 69–70.

11 Michèle Bernstein, *Tous les chevaux du roi* (Paris, 2004), p. 19.

12 Ibid., p. 22.

13 Ibid., p. 26.

14 Blaise Cendrars, *To the End of the World* (London, 2002), pp. 13, 73.

15 *The Complete Poems of François Villon* (New York, 1960), p. 25.

16 Ibid., p. 173.

17 Pierre Mac Orlan, *Petit manuel du parfait aventurier* (Paris, 1998), p. 15.

18 Guy Debord, *Panegyric*, vol. I, trans. James Brook (London, 1991), p. 46; *Panégyrique*, vol. I (Paris, 1993), p. 52–3.

19 Louis Chevalier, *The Assassination of Paris* (Chicago, 1994), p. 12.

20 Ibid., p. 246.

21 Ibid., p. 84.

22 'In Girum Imus Nocte et Consumimur Igni', pp. 226–7.

23 Chevalier, *Assassination of Paris*, p. 245.

24 *Guy Debord présente Potlatch, 1954–1957* (Paris, 1996), p. 38.

25 Ibid., pp. 37–9.

26 'Critique de la séparation', in Debord, *Oeuvres cinématographiques complètes*, p. 45.

27 Ibid., p. 46.

28 Ibid., pp. 55–6.

29 Ibid., p. 47.

30 Guy Debord, 'Perspectives de modifications conscientes dans la vie quotidienne', cited in *Internationale Situationniste* (Paris, 1997), p. 219.

31 Karl Marx, 'The Economic and Philosophical Manuscripts of 1844', in *Karl Marx: Early Writings* (Harmondsworth, 1974).

32 See the footnote to Debord's letter to Constant (25 May 1960) in Guy Debord, *Correspondance*, vol. I: *Juin 1957–août 1960* (Paris, 1999), p. 336.

33 Constant's early sketches of New Babylon, dating between 1956 and 1974, have been collated and presented in Catherine de Zegher and Mark Wigley, *The Activist Drawing: Retracing Situationist Architectures from Constant's New Babylon to Beyond* (Cambridge, MA, 2001).

34 'Programme elementaire du Bureau d'Urbanisme Unitaire', in *Internationale Situationniste*, p. 216.

35 'In Girum Imus Nocte et Consumimur Igni', in *Oeuvres cinematographiques complètes*, pp. 278–9.

36 Ibid., p. 280.

37 Philippe Sollers, 'L'etrange vie de Guy Debord', in *Eloge de l'infini* (Paris, 2002), p. 574.

38 'In Girum Imus Nocte et Consumimur Igni', in *Oeuvres cinematographiques complètes*, p. 240.

39 Ibid., p. 238.

40 Ibid., p. 247.

41 Ibid., p. 253.

42 Ibid., p. 259.

3 It Never Said Anything Extreme

1 Guy Debord, *La Société du spectacle* (Paris, 1992), p. 15.

2 Karl Marx, 'The Economic and Philosophical Manuscripts of 1844', in *Karl Marx: Early Writings* (Harmondsworth, 1974), p. 377.

3 Guy Debord, 'Avertissement pour la troisième édition française', in *La*

Société du Spectacle, p. 11.

4 Marx, *Economic and Philosophical Manuscripts of 1844*, p. 326.

5 Guy Debord, *Panégyrique*, vol. II (Paris, 1997).

6 Guy Debord, 'Préface à la quatrième édition italienne de *La Société du spectacle*', in *Commentaires sur 'La Société du spectacle'* (Paris, 1992), p. 131.

7 Guy Debord, *Considérations sur l'assassinat de Gérard Lebovici* (Paris, 1993), pp. 30–31.

8 'Préface à la quatrième édition italienne', p. 129.

9 This latter phrase Debord used to conclude an essay called 'La Planète malade' (1971), destined for the unlucky thirteenth *Internationale Situationniste* before its dissolution. In it, Debord tackles 'spectacular pollution', where mass-commodity production and alienated labour has created a 'sick planet'. The hitherto unpublished text has recently been released, in *La Planète malade* (Paris, 2004).

10 Guy Debord, *The Veritable Split in the International*, trans. Lucy Forsyth (London, 1985), pp. 11–12 (emphasis in original).

11 Ibid., p. 11.

12 'Lefebvre on the Situationist International', *October*, 79 (Winter 1977), p. 81.

13 'The Beginning of an Era [1969]' in *Situationist International Anthology*, ed. and trans. Ken Knabb (Berkeley, CA, 1989), pp. 227–8 (emphasis in original).

14 See the 'Interview with Michèle Bernstein' cited in Christophe Bourseiller, *Vie et mort de Guy Debord, 1931–94* (Paris, 1999), pp. 258–9.

15 'Lefebvre on the Situationist International'.

16 Henri Lefebvre, *La Somme et le reste* (Geneva, 1973), p. 11; see, too, Andy Merrifield, *Henri Lefebvre: A Critical Introduction* (New York, 2005).

17 Guy Debord, Attila Kotányi and Raoul Vaneigem, 'Theses on the Paris Commune', in *Situationist International Anthology*, p. 314.

18 'Lefebvre on the Situationist International'.

19 Debord, 'La Société du spectacle', in *Oeuvres cinématographiques complètes, 1952–78* (Paris, 1994), p. 139.

20 Ibid., pp. 140–41.

21 Guy Debord, *Cette mauvaise réputation* (Paris, 1993), pp. 94–5.

22 Marx, of course, used the sobriquet in his satire of Napoleon III, *The Eighteenth Brumaire of Louis Bonaparte*. Crapulinski, which he borrowed

from a Heine poem, comes from the French word *crapule*, meaning intemperance, gluttony or drunkenness; it can also stand for a loafer or a scoundrel.

23 Guy Debord (with Gianfranco Sanguinetti), *The Veritable Split in the International*, p. 77.

24 Debord, *Considérations*, p. 64.

25 J.H.M. Salmon, *Cardinal de Retz: The Anatomy of a Conspirator* (London, 1970), p. 62.

4 Aesthete of Subversion

1 Gianfranco Sanguinetti, *The Real Report on the Last Chance to Save Capitalism in Italy* (Fort Bragg, CA, 1997), p. 52.

2 Ibid., p. 58 (emphasis in original).

3 Ibid., p. 75.

4 For further details of this and other Red Brigade activities, see Richard Drake, *The Revolutionary Mystique and Terrorism in Contemporary Italy* (Bloomington, IN, 1989).

5 Ibid., p. 71.

6 'Préface à la quatrième édition italienne de *La Société du spectacle*', in *Commentaires sur 'La Société du Spectacle'* (Paris, 1992), pp. 142–3.

7 Ibid., p. 127.

8 Ibid., p. 134

9 Guy Debord, *Panegyric*, vol. I, trans. James Brook (London, 1991), p. 47; *Panégyrique*, vol. I (Paris, 1993), p. 55.

10 *Panegyric*, vol. I, pp. 47–8; *Panégyrique*, vol. I, pp. 54–5.

11 Niccolò Machiavelli, *The Prince* (New York, 1963), p. 109.

12 Ibid., p. 76

13 Guy Debord, *Considérations sur l'assassinat de Gérard Lebovici* (Paris, 1993), p. 33.

14 Gérard Guégan, *Guy Debord est mort, le Che aussi. Et alors?* (Paris, 2001).

15 Debord, *Considérations*, p. 29.

16 Baldasar Castiglione, *The Book of the Courtier* (New York, 1959), p. 98.

17 Federico García Lorca, *In Search of Duende* (New York, 1955), p. 55.

18 Guy Debord, *Stances sur la mort de son père* (Cognac, 1996), pp. 74–5.

19 Ibid., p. 75.

20 Ibid., p. 71.

21 Ibid., p. 73.

22 Author's interview with Alice Debord, Champot, 23 July 2003. It was in
    fact Alice who introduced Debord to the writings of George Borrow.

23 George Borrow, *Lavengro: The Scholar, the Gypsy, the Priest* (London,
    1925), pp. 102–3.

24 Alice Becker-Ho, *Les Princes du Jargon* (Paris, 1994), p. 16.

25 Ibid., p. 40.

26 *L'Essence du Jargon*, p. 41.

27 Debord, *Considérations*, pp. 79–80.

28 Guy Debord, *Des contrats* (Cognac, 1995), p. 54. Emphasis in original.

29 Ibid., p. 54.

5 I Am Not Somebody Who Corrects Himself

1 Edgar Allan Poe, 'The Murders in the Rue Morgue', in *Selected Writings
   of Edgar Allan Poe* (Boston, MA, 1956), p. 155.

2 Gérard Lebovici, *Tout sur le personnage* (Paris, 1984), p. 46.

3 Guy Debord, *Considérations sur l'assassinat de Gérard Lebovici* (Paris,
   1985), p. 10.

4 Ibid., p. 11. This citation is actually Debord's *détournement* of a line from
   Pascal's *Pensées*.

5 Ibid., pp. 74.

6 Ibid., p. 42.

7 Ibid., p. 92.

8 Lebovici's murder was, in fact, the second death that really shook
   Debord. The first was Asger Jorn's, who had died of lung cancer a
   decade earlier. In the spring of 1973, Jorn, from a Jutland hospital, had
   written to the Debords at their rue Saint-Jacques address, advising
   them of his terminal illness. But they were already sojourning in
   Florence, and without a telephone. Debord learnt of his friend's death
   on 1 May 1973 from an obituary in *Le Monde*. When they returned to
   Paris several weeks later, Jorn's last unanswered letter was discovered
   amid the pile of awaiting mail.

9 Chateaubriand, *Mémoires d'Outre-Tombe* (Paris, 1966), p. 232.

10 Guy Debord, *Panegyric*, vol. I, trans. James Brook (London, 1991), p. 46;

Panégyrique, vol. 1 (Paris, 1993), p. 53.

11 Pierre Mac Orlan, *Domaine de l'ombre* (Paris, 2000), p. 161.

12 Pierre Mac Orlan, *Petit manuel du parfait aventurier* (Paris, 1998), p. 22.

13 Ibid., pp. 28–9.

14 Ibid., p. 57.

15 Pierre Mac Orlan, *La Vénus internationale* (Paris, 1923), pp. 236–7.

16 Guy Debord, *Comments on the Society of the Spectacle*, trans. Malcolm Imrie (London, 1990), p. 5. The emphasis is in Debord's original French text, *Commentaires sur 'La Société du Spectacle'* (Paris, 1992), p. 17.

17 Debord, 'Avertissement pour la troisème édition Française', in *La Société du Spectacle* (Paris, 1992), p. 7. Debord's original words are: 'Je ne suis pas quelqu'un qui se corrige.'

18 Ibid., p. 10 (emphasis in the original).

19 Ibid.

20 Debord, *Comments*, p. 9.

21 Ibid., p. 10.

22 Ibid., pp. 12–23.

23 Ibid., p. 16 (emphasis in original).

24 Ibid., p. 24.

25 Ibid., p. 67 (emphasis in original).

26 Debord, *Panegyric*, vol. 1, p. 66; *Panégyrique*, vol. 1, p. 73.

27 Debord, *Panegyric*, vol. 1, pp. 67–68; *Panégyrique*, vol. 1, p. 75.

28 Guy Debord, *Cette mauvaise réputation* (Paris, 1993), p. 14.

29 Ibid., p. 50.

30 Guy Debord, *Des contrats* (Cognac, 1995), p. 65.

31 These passages have been assembled in an interesting little collection called *Eloge de l'ivresse* ('In Praise of Drunkenness'), ed. Sébastien Lapaque and Jérôme Leroy (Paris, 2000), in which Debord shares space with the likes of Rabelais, Baudelaire, Rimbaud, Edgar Allan Poe and Omar Khayyám.

32 Debord, *Panegyric*, vol. 1, p. 36; *Panégyrique*, vol. 1, pp. 44–5. Debord's confession that he had never found time to write is poetic licence, needless to say. Over recent years, something that has become apparent is his prolific letter writing. Four volumes of his correspondance, dating from June 1957, are now available through Librairie Arthème Fayard, a veritable feast for Debordian fans. Two more volumes in the series, stretching to the very end of his life, are forthcoming.

33 The interview with Christophe Bourseiller is cited in his book, *Vie et mort de Guy Debord*.

34 Cited in 'Dérive à Champot, en Haute-Loire', *Libération, 1931–94*, 9 January 1995 (Paris, 1999), p. 35.

6 Land of Storms

1 Carl von Clausewitz, *On War* (New York, 1993), pp. 474–9.

2 Thesis #165, *La Société du spectacle* (Paris, 1992). Emphasis in original.

3 Debord, 'L'Architecture et le jeu', in *Potlatch*, 20 (30 May 1955); reprinted in *Guy Debord présente Potlatch, 1954–1957* (Paris, 1996), p. 158.

4 Johan Huizinga, *Homo Ludens: A Study of the Play Element in Culture* (Boston, MA, 1955), p. 206.

5 See Ibrahim Warde, 'Smiling Serfs of the New Economy', *Le Monde diplomatique* (March 2002), pp. 14–15.

6 Ibid.

7 Johan Huizinga, *The Waning of the Middle Ages* (New York, 1989), Chapter 2.

8 Alice Becker-Ho, *Du jargon héritier en Bastardie* (Paris, 2002), p. 161.

9 See Guy Debord, 'Sur *In Girum*' [1977]; reprinted in *In Girum Imus Nocte et Consumimur Igni: édition critique augmentée de notes diverses de l'auteur; suivi de ordures et décombres* (Paris, 1999), pp. 61–2.

10 Alice Becker-Ho, *Là s'en vont les seigneuries* (Paris, 2003), p. 36.

11 Ibid., p. 31.

12 Alice Becker-Ho, *D'azur au triangle vidé de sable* (Cognac, 1998).

13 Pierre Mac Orlan, *Petit manuel du parfait aventurier* (Paris, 1988), pp. 42, 37.

14 Pierre Mac Orlan, *Villes* (Paris, 1929), p. 212.

15 Becker-Ho, *D'azur au triangle*, p. 15.

16 Ibid., p. 24.

17 Ibid., p. 47.

18 G.W.F. Hegel, *The Phenomenology of Spirit*, trans. A. V. Miller (Oxford, 1977), p. 19. In that letter, signed with Patrick Mosconi, Alice said: 'there is nothing to yield a profit, nothing to rehabilitate, nor embellish nor falsify . . . There is nothing to inherit. It is Debord who ought to inherit Debord. The story ends there.'

19 Christophe Bourseiller, *Vie et mort de Guy Debord, 1931–94* (Paris, 1999), p. 525. This interesting and suggestive revelation about *My Dinner with André* elicits only a couple of throwaway lines and is never followed up by Bourseiller.

20 The screenplay of this remarkable film is available in book form: see Wallace Shawn and André Gregory, *My Dinner with André* (New York, 1981).

21 Ibid., pp. 93–4.

22 Ibid., pp. 94–5.

23 Ibid., p. 95.

Select Bibliography

Debord's books in French

Cette mauvaise réputation (Paris, 1993)
Commentaires sur 'La Société du Spectacle' (Paris, 1992)
Considérations sur l'assassinat de Gérard Lebovici (Paris, 1993)
Correspondance, vol. I: *Juin 1957–août 1960* (Paris, 1999)
Correspondance, vol. II: *Septembre 1960–décembre 1964* (Paris, 2001)
Correspondance, vol. III: *Janvier 1965–décembre 1968* (Paris, 2003)
Correspondance, vol. IV: *Janvier 1969–décembre 1972* (Paris, 2004)
Des contrats (Cognac, 1995)
Fin de Copenhague (Paris, 1986) [with Asger Jorn]
Guy Debord presente Potlatch, 1954–57 (Paris, 1996)
In Girum Imus Nocte et Consumimur Igni: édition critique augmentée de notes diverses de l'auteur; suivi de ordures et décombres (Paris, 1999)
La Déclin et la chute de l'economie spectaculaire marchande (Paris, 1993)
La Planète malade (Paris, 2004)
La Société du Spectacle (Paris, 1992)
La Véritable Scission dans l'Internationale Situationniste: édition augmentée (Paris, 1999) [with Gianfranco Sanguinetti]
Le 'Jeu de la Guerre': relevé des positions successives de toutes les forces au cours d'une partie (Paris, 1988) [with Alice Becker-Ho]
Le Marquis de Sade a des yeux de fille (Paris, 2004)
Mémoires, 1952–1953 (Paris, 1993) [with Asger Jorn]
Oeuvres cinématographiques complètes, 1952–78 (Paris, 1994)
Panégyrique, vol. I (Paris, 1993)
Panégyrique, vol. II (Paris, 1997)
Rapport sur la construction des situations et sur les conditions de l'organisation

et de l'action de la tendance Situationniste Internationale (Paris, 2000)
Stances sur la mort de son père (Cognac, 1996) [translation of Jorge Manrique]
Véridique rapport sur les dernières chances de sauver le capitalisme en Italie
    (Paris, 1976) [translation of Gianfranco Sanguinetti]

Debord's films

Critique de la séparation (1961). 20 minutes.
Guy Debord, son art et son temps (1994). 60 minutes [in collaboration with
    Brigitte Cornand]
Hurlements en faveur de Sade (1952). 75 minutes
In Girum Imus Nocte et Consumimur Igni (1978). 100 minutes
La Société du Spectacle (1973). 80 minutes
Réfutation de tous les jugements, tant élogieux qu'hostiles, qui ont été jusqu'ici
    portés sur le film 'La Société du Spectacle' (1975). 25 minutes
Sur le passage de quelques personnes à travers une assez courte unité de temps
    (1959). 20 minutes
On Debord: *Guy Debord: une étrange guerre* (2000). 45 minutes [by Philippe
    Sollers and Emmanuel Descombes]

Debord's books in English translation

Comments on 'The Society of the Spectacle', trans. Malcolm Imrie (London,
    1990)
Complete Cinematic Works of Guy Debord, trans. Ken Knabb (Oakland, CA,
    2003)
Considerations on the Assassination of Gérard Lebovici, trans. Robert Greene
    (Los Angeles, CA, 2001)
Panegyric, vol. I, trans. James Brook (London, 1991)
Panegyric, 2 vols, trans. James Brook and John McHale (London, 2004)
The Real Split in the Situationist International, trans. John McHale (London,
    2003)
The Society of the Spectacle, trans. Fredy Perlman and John Supak (Detroit,
    1970; London, 1977); *The Society of the Spectacle*, trans. Donald
    Nicholson-Smith (New York, 1994)

Books on Debord in French

Jean-Marie Apostolidès, *Les Tombeaux de Guy Debord* (Paris, 1999)
Christophe Bourseiller, *Vie et mort de Guy Debord, 1931–94* (Paris, 1999)
Boris Donné, *Pour memoires: un essai d'élucidation des memoires de Guy Debord* (Paris, 2004)
Shigenobu Gonzalvez, *Guy Debord ; ou, la beauté du négatif* (Paris, 1998)
Cécile Guilbert, *Pour Guy Debord* (Paris, 1996)
Vincent Kaufmann, *Guy Debord: La révolution au service de la poésie* (Paris, 2001)

Books on Debord in English

Len Bracken, *Guy Debord, Revolutionary: A Critical Biography* (Venice, CA, 1997)
Andrew Hussey, *The Game of War: The Life and Death of Guy Debord* (London, 2001)
Anselm Jappe, *Guy Debord* (Berkeley, CA, 1999)

Situationist and related texts in French

Archives et documents situationnistes (Paris, 2003)
Alice Becker-Ho, *D'azur au triangle vidé de sable* (Cognac, 1998)
—, *Là s'en vont les seigneuries* (Cognac, 2003)
—, *Les Princes du Jargon* (Paris, 1990)
Michèle Bernstein, *Tous les chevaux du roi* (Paris, 2004)
Laurent Chollet, ed., *Les Situationnistes: l'utopie incarnée* (Paris, 2004)
Débat d'orientation de l'ex-internationale situationniste (Paris, 1974) [also Éditions du Cercle Carré, 2000]
Jean-Luc Douin, *Les Jours obscurs de Gérard Lebovic* (Paris, 2004)
Internationale situationniste, 1958–1969 (Paris, 1997)
Sébastien Lapaque and Jérôme Leroy, *Eloge de l'ivresse: d'Anacréon à Guy Debord* (Paris, 2000)
Gérard Lebovici, *Tout sur le personnage* (Paris, 1984)
Jean-François Martos, *Histoire de l'internationale situationniste* (Paris, 1989)

Jean-Michel Mension, *La Tribu* (Paris, 1998)
Ralph Rumney, *Le Consul* (Paris, 1999)
Textes et documents situationnistes, 1957–1960 (Paris, 2003)
René Viénet, *Enragés et situationnistes dans le mouvement des occupations* (Paris, 1998)

Situationist and related texts in English

Dark Star Collective, *Beneath the Paving Stones: Situationists and the Beach, May 1968* (Oakland, CA, 2001)
Christopher Gray, ed., *Leaving the Twentieth Century: The Incomplete Work of the Situationist International* (London, 1998)
Ken Knabb, ed., *Situationist International Anthology: Bureau of Public Secrets* (Berkeley, CA, 1989)
Tom McDonough, ed., *Guy Debord and the Situationist International: Texts and Documents* (Cambridge, MA, 2002)
Greil Marcus, *Lipstick Traces: A Secret History of the Twentieth Century* (Cambridge, MA, 1989)
Sadie Plant, *The Most Radical Gesture: The Situationist International in a Postmodern Age* (London, 1992)
Simon Sadler, *The Situationist City* (Cambridge, MA, 1998)
Elizabeth Sussman, ed., *On the Passage of a Few People through a Rather Brief Moment in Time: The Situationist International, 1957–1972* (Cambridge and Boston, MA, 1989)
René Viénet, *Enragés and Situationists in the Occupation Movement, May '68* (London, 1992)

Situationists on the web

http://www.notbored.org
http://www.bopsecrets.org
http://www.cddc.vt.edu/sionline/notes.html

Acknowledgements

I've been lucky to encounter several people who kept me rolling with this project. Thanks to Jeff Byles and Malcolm Imrie, who read earlier versions of the text and offered wise words of encouragement and informed criticism, as did Vivian Constantinopoulos at Reaktion. I'm grateful to Alice Debord, who welcomed me to Champot, offered me wine, and graciously answered questions about her late husband; ditto those Champot and Bellevue-la-Montagne locals, particularly Pierre Berthier, Marcel Allibert and Madame Soulier, who tolerated my periodic intrusions with good cheer; Mazen Labban, François Maheux, Daniel Niles and Erik Swyngedouw, fellow Debordian voyagers, shared my mad passions; Eric Comstock provided the romantic soundtrack and Neil Brenner the whole food; and Corinna, my *compagnon de route*, not only stood by me in this storm-tossed adventure, she invariably took the helm on a journey that continues to flow – upstream, against the current, beside the Allier river.

Photo Acknowledgements

The author and publishers wish to express their thanks to the following sources of illustrative material and/or permission to reproduce it:

Photos by the author: pp. 8, 9, 112, 115, 117, 135; photo courtesy of the Netherlands Architectural Institute: p. 28; photos Roger Viollet/ Rex Features: pp. 41 (rv-90996), 71 (rv-357418N).